KT-437-571

Contents

Part 3: Computers in education

Preface

THE LEARNING CENTRE
HAMMERSMITH AND WEST
LONDON COLLEGE
GLIDDON ROAD
LONDON W14 9BL
0181 741 1688

In March 1995 the Children's Play Council (formerly the National Voluntary Council for Children's Play) organised a conference on children and new technology, held at the National Children's Bureau. At this conference, leading professionals in key fields assessed the ways that children were engaging with new technology, and discussed the consequences of these patterns of use – for children themselves, for families and for society as a whole. The conference stemmed from the Council's interest in television, videos and computer games as an aspect of children's play and recreation. But children use new technology not only for recreation, but also for learning. Hence it was decided to broaden the scope of the event to include educational applications of computers, so as to give a more complete picture of children's experience of new technology. Unusually, the conference also gave children the chance to describe their experiences and express their opinions, with presentations from eight comprehensive school pupils.

This book organises the papers from the original conference around three themes. The first part focuses on children watching television and videos, the second examines children's use of computer games and the third looks at computers in education. Introductory sections to each part set the papers in context and summarise their arguments, with the help of extracts from the schoolchildren's presentations. Of course, each of these issues has been the subject of a vast amount of research and analysis, which it would be almost impossible to survey in a single publication. But this is not the aim of *Electronic Children*. Rather, it aims to provide a set of perspectives, a series of contrasting but interconnecting views over a landscape.

Tim Gill
January 1996

Acknowledgements

On behalf of the Children's Play Council, I want to thank all the contributors whose papers are included here and who spoke at the original 'Electronic Children' conference. I also want to thank the children from Graveney Secondary School in South London who spoke so impressively: Natalie Blackburne, Elizabeth Dwomoh, Victor John, Debbie Lovell, Natasha Mudhar, Shem Pennant, Joel Prager and Alex Woodcraft. Thanks also to the conference team at the National Children's Bureau and to Anna Lubelska, programme director of the Council and the driving force behind the event. Anne Weyman and Fiona Blakemore at the Bureau encouraged me to develop the conference proceedings into book form, giving useful advice along the way. Special thanks are also due to AST Computer, for their generous support of the publication of this book. The contributors are responsible for their texts, and any views expressed elsewhere are mine; they should not be taken to represent the views of either the Council or the Bureau.

Notes on contributors

Mark Allerton was a primary school teacher in London for six years. He has worked in child development research since 1992. His work includes research into the development of mathematical concepts. His contribution to this volume is based on research into children's emotional responses to television, funded by the Broadcasting Standards Council. He is currently working on a study of the effects of bereavement on children.

Dr Charles Crook is Reader in Psychology at Loughborough University School of Human Sciences. He received his PhD in Psychology from Cambridge University. He has held research psychology posts at Strathclyde University in Scotland and at Brown University and the University of California at San Diego in the United States. Since 1983 he has been involved in numerous research projects concerned with computers in education. Some of these have been based in primary schools and some have involved undergraduate level work. His particular interest has been in how new technology can support collaborative and other socially-organised styles of learning. He has published numerous papers on this topic including coediting the book *Computers, Cognition and Development* published by Wiley in 1987. In 1994 Routledge published his book *Computers and the Collaborative Experience of Learning* in which most of his own recent empirical work is summarised – converging on an integrated account of how computers can support a strongly interpersonal model of teaching and learning.

Tim Gill has been policy officer for the Children's Play Council (formerly the National Voluntary Council for Children's Play) since October 1994. He is the author of the Council's publication *Playing for Local Government*, and has previously worked in community information, voluntary sector management development and social research. He is currently reading for a Masters degree in Philosophy at Birkbeck College, University of London, exploring the ways that adults and children learn to understand the world and their place in it.

Dr Mark Griffiths is a chartered psychologist and senior lecturer from Nottingham Trent University. Since 1988 his research has concentrated on gaming addictions and he is best known for his work on fruit machine addiction. His first book on this subject, *Adolescent Gambling*, came out in 1995, and he is currently writing his second book, *Technological Addictions*, which will concentrate heavily on computer games.

Professor Elizabeth Newson was Director of the Child Development Research Unit at the University of Nottingham before retiring from that post in August 1994. She is now Emeritus Professor there, but has a new career at the Early Years Diagnostic Centre, Nottinghamshire, specialising in children with communication disorders. Her long term work on child rearing in social contexts has included both children with disabilities and 'ordinary children' and she has produced many books which emphasise a language of partnership between professionals and parents.

Libby Purves is a writer and broadcaster. Her non-fiction publications include *How Not To Be a Perfect Mother*, *How Not To Be a Perfect Child* and *How Not To Be the Perfect Family*, and she has also written two novels, *Casting Off* and *A Long Walk in the Wintertime*. She is the presenter of Midweek on Radio 4 and is a *Times* columnist and feature writer.

Helen Rickards graduated in 1989 from Cambridge with a B.Ed. She worked as deputy IT coordinator in a Suffolk middle school for two years and then moved to the English Montessori school in Madrid where she developed her interest in IT and bilingual pupils. After two years abroad Helen read for an MA in IT in Education at the University of Reading where her research focused on how hypermedia could enhance the learning of pupils with learning difficulties. Helen is currently working as IT coordinator at a Cambridgeshire primary school and is a member of the British Computer Society Schools' Committee.

Elizabeth Stutz's interest in play is of long standing, first having observed German children in 1945–6 when she formed a group of ex-Hitler Youth in her spare time while working with the US Army of Occupation in Germany. Later, when teaching in a variety of schools in Britain, starting at the prep school for Gordonstoun and other independent schools, she noted throughout the effects that various kinds of play, as well as lack of play, had on the development of children. As a result she set up one of the original CSE courses in child development in the 1960s. In 1990–92, she undertook two studies of out-of-school activities of children in Norwich, with special reference to the decline in spontaneous play and increase in violent behaviour observed.

Colin Wells taught Computing and Maths in a Kent secondary school for ten years, including pioneering work with early microcomputers in the late 1970s. This led him to be Technical Director of a Research and Development group in Plymouth, writing computer programs and developing IT support materials and courses for teachers in a wide range of subject areas. He then became founder/Manager of the Microtechnology Unit of the Music Education Centre at Reading University – again developing materials and training support for music teachers in the use of IT. He is currently Senior Lecturer in IT in Education at Reading University, where he is Course Director of the Masters Degree Course in IT in Education. Colin has wide ranging qualifications, particularly in Computing, Maths and Music, and is active with the British Computer Society (BCS), being Chairman of the Quality of IT in Schools group. He was previously Chairman of the Schools' Committee and Council member, and also BCS representative on JAPONITE (Joint Advisory Panel on IT in Education) which meets regularly with the Minister for Education.

Foreword

In 1995 AST Computer sponsored the National Children's Bureau's 'Electronic Children' conference, which aimed to investigate the effects of technology on children. The conference brought home the tremendous benefits that PCs can offer children both for their academic work and for their own personal development.

Our active support of this event and the subsequent book of the same title, demonstrate AST's commitment to supporting children's causes. We are keen to encourage debate on, and understanding of, the potential of computers, both in education and for a young person's personal development.

As the number one supplier of personal computers in all our retail outlets, AST is a key player in the UK home computer market. Consequently, we are extremely interested in keeping close to any developments and issues that are affecting families, and hence their children, who use personal computers in the home. Recent research has shown that one in four of the UK's 22 million households can boast ownership of a personal computer. By the end of this year, this number is forecast to rise to 29 per cent – nearly one in three homes.[1]

In other words, technology has arrived in the British home and is here to stay. There are hundreds of software packages aimed at the family with a PC. Parents and their children have access to computers in the office and school, if not in their own home. Perhaps unlike their parents, children today are fully immersed in technology and are not afraid to explore its potential.

Graham Hopper, AST Computer

---

[1] (*These figures are from Ziff-Davis and were presented at the launch of their new home computer title* Computer Life).

Introduction
A view from the middle generation

Libby Purves

I write as a lay person and a mother; mother of a considerable computer buff aged twelve and honorary aunt to any number of jumping little electronic figures of Supermario, who haunted my kitchen for two whole years, banging his head enthusiastically on brick ceilings, in a manner disturbingly reminiscent of my own career. Detailed expertise is something that other contributors will give you: on everything from the health of computer gamesters to the violence of television and the desirability of children surfing the global information highway. All I offer are some sideways looks at the way we, parents and teachers of the middle generation, look at these things.

Back in the 1960s, there was a science fiction story about some strange packets which fall from the sky into remote rural areas. The locals open them, find coloured rods and cubes and toys, and give them to the children. The children fool around, get more and more absorbed, then suddenly start asking odd mathematical questions. Eventually – you guessed it – disaster: the children vanish into another dimension. Emotionally distanced, they have been taken up by the alien intelligence and induced to join it, up there somewhere. It was a brilliant story, echoing the old fear of demonic possession and Pied Pipers, and the new fear of a computer future. It still raises a shudder. If you grew up with black and white TV, there is something eerie and worrying about the sight of a small face, bathed in the unearthly glow of a VDU. Oh woe, we cry – Sonic the Hedgehog is stealing my baby's soul! We feel like illiterate immigrants to the new world, marvelling helplessly over the brilliance of our educated children, but at the same time afraid that they will be taken away from the old culture, the old values.

I think we should be braver, and more optimistic. Computers and CD–ROMs are just an expansion of the ways in which knowledge and entertainment are transmitted; but they are only things, only tools. There were probably people around in Caxton's time who predicted that the printing press would lead to the end of conversation and public speaking: it didn't. And electronics will not kill books, either. Teenagers are computer buffs, yet teen fiction is the biggest growth area in publishing. It probably won't even kill newspapers; much is said about the 'electronic newspaper' in which you download the items from a computer programmed to pick only the ones that you want to read. But who knows what they want to read, before they get browsing? The human factor will always demand randomness, surprises, the tactile pleasure of turning a new page.

I collected stories, while thinking about this subject. One newspaper firmly asserts that the day of the computer game is gone, that Sonic and Supermario have had their chips: it quotes 'none of the kids are playing them any more.' The same paper two days later claimed that the reason boys do measurably worse than girls at school is that – wait for it – boys play computer games, and are therefore distracted. There is presumably no distraction on offer for girls, and all those posters of pop stars are academically highly useful...!

Here are some other stories from the media: 'lack of computers in schools is threatening our children's education and development', 'computers in schools are threatening the social development of children, alienating them from their peers and reducing respect for their teachers', 'early learning can be promoted by electronic games'; 'smart parents are scrambling to buy their two-year-olds a first computer, lest they miss out', 'electronic toys are stunting the capacity of children to play creatively with ordinary objects', 'worry about whether schools are keeping up with networking'; 'not enough of them are on the Internet'! Education is threatened, we'll all fall behind Europe and be doomed to third class citizenship forever!

Whereas in the next magazine I pick up there is an interview with Stephen Fry, just before he vanished...about his Internet hobby, and how you can dial up alt.pornography or alt.masturbation, and download pictures of Wayne Bobbitt's severed bits if you want; and an account of new measures being taken against the child pornography file on the Internet – people sending foul paedophile material on alt.sex.intergen.

All this conveys a general sense that if the batteries run out, we're all doomed; and if they don't, we're all zombies. It echoes and reinforces that feeling we have, of being peasants unable to keep up with our own children. In the face of these feelings, we ought to look more critically, objectively, and yes, relaxedly, at what is really happening.

Technology is a tool. Computers and video screens are *things:* not gods, not even people. They are, admittedly, powerful channels, by which offensive and ill-intentioned people can communicate with our children. But so are public parks, and railway trains, and books and comics. They are also absorbing pursuits, which if used unwisely can waste children's learning time and stunt their healthy physical development. But then, so are bar-billiard tables, and smoking, and all night discos, and even athletics...and we have found ways of limiting those, and getting the best out of them while avoiding the worst.

We must not get paranoid about new technology. Computer addiction may exist, but it is a great rarity: far more common is the situation, as Noelle Janis Norton puts it, of parents who have forgotten they can say no, enough. Children who play at anything for thirty hours a week ought to be dissuaded, just as our generation was told to put its books away and go out in the fresh air. Of course, some children do flee into computer games from home or school difficulties...but they have to have the difficulties to flee from.

If there are alternatives – if there is grass, and open space, and ropes to swing on, and dogs to throw sticks for – believe me, children will do it. I have had hordes of them around me for some years now. I am well aware that often there isn't grass and open space, and bikes and ropes. But should we blame the computer, if we have built a society and designed cities where our children have nothing more interesting to do? Or nothing safe, anyway? The computer has replaced TV as babysitter in many homes; at least children using it are active, at least one finger is, and their brain. And if we would rather they were out in green spaces, we should fight to provide those, not blame the computer.

As to the games themselves, children find games to suit their personalities. Sim City is constructive and intelligent; many others are tactical, strategic, interesting. Some are senselessly violent: but it is an idle parent, copping out, who doesn't even try to find out. If you ask someone who their babysitter is, they don't say 'Oh, some guy...'. They know the name, references, everything. If you ask what their child is doing, though, they say 'Oh...computer games' – but it could be Robocop, it could be sexual violence, it could be town planning. This education of us, the parents, is a vital brick in the edifice of building a decent relationship with technology for our children: schools also have a responsibility to update us, to educate us, to let us get hands-on and try to understand our children's new world. And to bring our values to bear on it.

For, I say again, computers are things. Morally neutral things. If you have a brick, you can smash someone's face with it, or use it to build a cathedral. The choice is yours, not the thing's. Technology does not change essential ethical and moral values. Read the book *Disclosure*, on which the recent hit film was based. Michael Crichton is a subtle writer, fascinated by technology, but here, as in *Jurassic Park*, the message he gives us is that human greed and stupidity is the real enemy. Although the solution to the mystery at the centre of the book involves a state of the art virtual reality machine, the real answer is that his colleague has been incompetent, covered it up, lied and cheated and tried to get him sacked for her mistake. Behaviour doesn't change: only the tools. The only harm which will come to us is if we are afraid of new gadgets, refuse to learn about them, and leave them as weapons in the hands of a few enthusiasts we cannot necessarily trust. Make them our servants, and they can never be the masters.

Part 1: Children watching television

Introduction

Tim Gill

Children watch a wide range of television and video, for all sorts of reasons. There are many interesting questions one could ask about this, but for almost as long as television has been around, the main concern has been about its effects. When it comes to television, it is the media effects debate that provokes the most empassioned arguments (and the greatest media coverage).

The basic positions in the debate are as follows. On one side, many psychologists assert that there is clear evidence that exposure to violent images from television and video does make some children more violent. Thus in a recent review, Ellen Wartella writes:

> there is evidence...that heavy viewing of television violence in the early grade school years is associated with criminal behaviour among young adults. (Wartella, 1995)

This is the view Elizabeth Newson defends in her contribution, and she concludes that we must 'restrict such material from home viewing'.

Against this view other researchers, mainly from the field of media studies but including some psychologists, argue that children are not made more violent by watching violence on screen. Thus, a review of much of the same research as Newson concludes that 'the attempts to find direct effects of television on viewers' behaviour have had no success' (Gauntlett, 1995).

Readers who wish to examine the evidence further should refer to the material cited. But in addition to assessing this evidence, there are interesting questions to be asked about the way the debate is conducted. What models are being used to explain children's engagement with television and video? What does this engagement mean for children? What relevant changes are taking place elsewhere in children's lives? In sum, where might there be gaps in the story? Children are not like rats in a laboratory; if they are being affected by the images they see and hear, we would expect more to be taking place than unthinking mimicry.

Mark Allerton's paper explores some of these issues. His research looks at how children and parents respond to television. His findings show that children from six to 16 years of age interact actively with television images. 'The meaning that children ascribe to the images they see...will determine how they cope with any stress it causes', he writes. Moreover, children fully appreciate the difference between fact and fiction, and find real-life images just as upsetting as fictional ones, if not more so. In Allerton's model of children's engagement with media, children are able to analyse and assess the images they see and the messages they receive. In another paper on the same research he states that 'children develop a literacy for reading television just as they do for books' (Allerton, 1995). By contrast, according to Wartella (1995):

> current theorizing suggests that portrayals of violence operate to encode, maintain and evoke violent ideas, thoughts and behavioural scripts in heavy viewers which are later acted out in a variety of settings

– a much more impoverished model of children's engagement.

Are children in general becoming more violent? Well, yes, it seems they are (with the usual caveats about the interpretation of crime statistics). Oliver James, a psychologist, examined figures for juvenile crime, and especially violent crime, in the last 50 years or so, and found a dramatic increase in violent crimes since 1987, in the context of a wider drop in juvenile crime (James, 1995). He in fact attributes this to greater poverty and the growth of a 'winner–loser' culture that encourages violent responses from young men in the poorest sections of society; he does not consider the possible effects of easy access to violent videos and media images. Indeed no serious research has yet been published that relates the alleged increase in levels of juvenile violent crime to media effects.

In 1995 a commission set up by the Calouste Gulbenkian Foundation reported its findings on the causes and extent of violence involving children. The commission, comprising distinguished academics, practitioners and writers, found that 'the most potent of the risk factors are clearly sited in childhood and within the family' (Calouste Gulbenkian Foundation, 1995). With respect to the media effects debate (which the report usefully summarises) the commission concludes that 'the context in which the child views violent images...is likely to influence whether or how the child is affected.' Its recommendations support stricter adherence to existing classification systems, watersheds and guidelines, as well as for 'increased critical understanding by pupils of the new communications technologies'.

Video violence and the protection of children

Elizabeth Newson

Background

In February 1994 I was invited to write a discussion paper to be circulated to all members of the House of Commons and the House of Lords, at a time when there was an opportunity to consider the implications of video violence in relation to the Criminal Justice Bill. Obviously, to accept this invitation was to involve taking a hard look at the evidence for a connection between the violent images which children see on screen and their own violent behaviour. However, this was something I already felt the need to do, prompted by the reverberations of the tragic James Bulger case, and the media demands that were already being made on me as a developmental psychologist to comment on what might have led two ten-year-old children to murder a two-year-old in cold blood.

The discussion paper was circulated in March 1994, and attracted considerable public attention. Since it was widely misquoted, although later published in several academic and professional journals, I propose here to give it in its original form and then to add a few remarks on some of the criticisms that were made at the time, though amid widespread support. For background information, I have also added an *aide-mémoire* which I prepared for the Home Affairs Committee who subsequently took evidence in this area.

Introduction

Two-year-old James Bulger was brutally and sadistically murdered in February 1993 by two ten-year-old children. This stark fact has prompted a long overdue focus upon what conditions in our society could precipitate such an unthinkable action.

The need to ask 'why?' is central to the human condition; we cannot and should not accept a randomness in events, unless we

9

are content to see the world spin totally out of our control. As is usual at such times, during the trial the media approached every possible 'expert' for comments on causes; and as usual the experts obliged, from their various points of view, sometimes under pressure with little time for the consideration that was due. Then, once again as usual, other media commentators derided the multiplicity of views, and with it the entire search for causes.

Now that the immediate shock of the trial has a little receded, perhaps this is the time to evaluate more carefully the situation which this murder of a child by children has forced us to examine. Many have asked despairingly how we can ever come to terms with it. We can only begin to do so by facing it squarely and considering what might be done: not to erase Jamie's loss, not to redeem the two children who survive, but to try to ensure that Jamie is not just the first of many such victims. And, given that children of ten are by law seen as in need of protection by society, we perhaps should consider future Roberts and Jons, and how far society should accept some responsibility for children who, at least in some sense, are its victims themselves.

It is of course more comforting to believe that children like Robert Thompson and Jon Venables are a 'one-off': 'evil freaks', as some sections of the Press described them. Detective-Sergeant Phil Roberts, present at Robert's interviews and in desperate need of comfort himself, was quoted as saying: 'These two were freaks who just found each other. You should not compare these two boys with other boys – they were evil' (*Independent*, 25 November 1993). Similarly, one might describe a child who lacked any sense of pity or moral control as the equivalent of an adult psychopath; but does it not defy belief that *two* such children 'just found each other'?

Whoever might or might not have been leader – however much this might have been a case of two children egging each other on – the fact is that this was not a crime of sudden impulse. Jamie was not the first toddler that these children attempted to entice away that day; they both persevered in seeking a victim. If they had actually pushed Jamie into traffic or into the canal, both of which they explicitly considered, then we might have seen such an action as an uncontrolled and perhaps one-sided impulse; they rejected both these ideas, and it is in fact the sustained determination with which they propelled a distressed and frightened little boy over two-and-a-half miles, stopping when necessary to 'explain themselves' to concerned enquirers, that is another piece of evidence that an act of torture was in the making. We now know that the final scene beside the railway line was long-drawn-out and merciless; that paint was thrown, and blows were struck not once but enough to cause 42 separate injuries; that there were sexual elements to the torture and Jamie's mouth was damaged on the inside; and that the children got blood on the soles of their shoes.

These details have to be remembered, much as one would like to forget them, because of what they imply: that in this crime there was both the expectation and the attainment of _satisfaction_ of some sort through doing deliberate and sustained violence to a very small child (described *by the children* as a 'baby') whose distress was unremitting. Afterwards, too, the children were composed enough first to push James on to a railway line in an attempt to disguise the murder, then to wander down to the video shop where they were known and where their demeanour did not arouse suspicion of anything worse than truancy, even in their mothers.

So here is a crime that we could all wish had been perpetrated by 'evil freaks'; but already the most cursory reading of the news since then suggests that it is not a 'one-off'. Shortly after this trial, children of similar age in Paris were reported to have set upon a tramp, encouraged by another tramp, kicked him and thrown him down a well. In England an adolescent girl was tortured by her 'friends' over days, using direct soundtrack quotations from a horror video (*Child's Play 3*) as part of her torment, and was eventually set on fire and thus killed; while the following note appeared in a local paper on 7 December 1993:

> Two schoolboys were today expected to appear in court accused of torturing a six-year-old on a railway line. The youngsters, aged ten and eleven, allegedly tried to force the boy to electrocute himself on a track in Newcastle upon Tyne last week. They are also accused of stabbing him in the arm with a knife. They will appear before Gosforth Youth Court in Newcastle upon Tyne charged with making threats to kill and three offences of indecently assaulting the youngster and his two brothers aged seven and ten.

(Since this paper was written there have been other such crimes: notably, the kicking to death of a five-year-old Norwegian girl by three six-year-old 'playmates' in October 1994. In the same month, two 10- and 11-year-old children killed a five-year-old in Chicago by suspending and then dropping him from a high-rise car park when he would not steal sweets for them.)

We do not have the information to be able to comment on the

full background of any of these crimes at present: all that can be said is that they have in common a willingness of two or more children or adolescents together to carry out brutally violent assaults likely to result in protracted suffering and death.

It would be quite unlikely that any single cause for these children's behaviour could be identified, although possible contributing factors might be offered; for instance, experts consulted by *The Independent* (25 November 1993) variously suggested the effects of physical abuse, severe emotional neglect resulting in lack of self-worth, deprivation, 'play on the mean side which went too far', exposure to sadistic videos and conversations, sexual abuse and disturbed family relationships. Poverty and despair related to unemployment and a culture of no-hope families have also been cited. However, child abuse, poverty and neglect have been a part of many children's experiences over the years; indeed, although neither Jon nor Robert could be said to have come from happy and nurturant homes, there was little evidence of the extremes of neglect and abuse that could be documented in any social services department. What, then, can be seen as the 'different' factor that has entered the lives of countless children and adolescents in recent years? This has to be recognised as the easy availability to children of gross images of violence on video.

Evidence of professional concern

Over the past few years, considerable anxiety has been expressed by those professionally concerned with children about the effects of horror, sex and violence, soft porn and similar scenes experienced by children via videos seen in their own or their friends' homes. Mr Justice Brown identified children's access to sadistic videos as cause for concern following the Rochdale case of suspected ritual abuse, where the children's familiarity with horror images from videos such as *Nightmare on Elm Street* misled social workers into assuming that they must have experienced such things in reality. At an early stage the British Paediatric Association had invited comments from its members on damaging effects of 'video nasties': at that time, concern was mainly centred upon children who were presenting with nightmares and traumatisation by images that they could not erase from their minds; and one might suggest that this was an 'innocent' period, in that having nightmares is a relatively healthy reaction, denoting the child's continuing sensitivity to such images.

More recently, however, concern has grown greater and has addressed more serious and long-lasting effects. It now seems that professionals in child health and psychology underestimated the degree of brutality and sustained sadism that film-makers were capable of inventing and willing to portray, let alone the special-effects technologies which would support such images; and we certainly underestimated how easy would be children's access to them. Where formerly children were said to see them 'by accident' or in defiance of parental edict, it is now clear that many children watch adult-only videos on a regular basis, with or without their parents' knowledge, and that many parents make less than strenuous efforts to restrict their children's viewing. Thus it is not surprising that Mr Justice Morland speculated upon the part that such videos might have played in creating the degree of desensitisation to compassion that the children in the Bulger case showed – not only during their attack, but in comments like Robert's (before he admitted to the killing): 'if I wanted to kill a baby, I would kill my own, wouldn't I?'. (Note that neither I nor other professionals have suggested that any single video caused Jamie's death: we are talking about a steady diet of such material.)

There must be special concern when children (or adults, for that matter) are repeatedly exposed to images of vicious cruelty in the context of *entertainment and amusement*. Michael Medved makes the point:

> Not only do these films suggest that brute force is a prerequisite for manliness, that physical intimidation is irresistibly sexy, and that violence offers an effective solution to all human problems; today's movies also advance the additional appalling idea that the most appropriate response to the suffering of others is sadistic laughter. (Medved, 1992)

In the context of entertainment:

- The viewer receives the implicit message that *this is all good fun* – something with which to while away one's leisure time.
- The *child* viewer receives distorted images of emotions that he has not yet experienced so must accept – especially dangerous where love, sex and violence are equated.
- The ingenuity with which brutality is portrayed is likely to escalate over time, since the entertainment industry must try to be more and more 'entertaining' and must allow for jaded palates. (How far this might go in the future in terms

of video games and virtual reality is not within the scope of this paper.)

● So that viewers will not be too disturbed to experience 'entertainment', the victims must be portrayed as being somewhat subhuman, so that they need not be pitied.

● An alternative is that they should be portrayed as *deserving* violent treatment. Robert and Jon explained that they had had to go on throwing bricks at Jamie (30 blows with bricks and an iron bar were counted) because he kept on getting up. (This resonates with the attitudes of many abusive parents, who testify that they *had to* hit the baby because she would keep on crying.) A parallel in a recently released film is where we witness in lit silhouette the multiple rape of a woman by a queue of men, and hear her agonised screams, all in the context of an intent to punish her.

The connection between viewing violence and change in attitudes or behaviour

The principle that what is experienced vicariously will have *some* effect on *some* people is an established one, and is the reason why industry finds it worth while to spend millions of pounds on advertising. Medved (1992) has pointed out that an advertising campaign will be regarded as a major success on the basis of a quite small percentage of its viewers changing their buying habits. The derisive question which film-makers have put to their critics, 'have *you* been tempted to become a serial killer by watching our films?' is disingenuous: it ignores differing stability, susceptibility to influence and levels of immaturity among the audience as a whole. We know that children can be traumatised, not only by the images they see, but also by additional images that are suggested by their imagination in response to the originals; but far more dangerous, because more lastingly damaging, would be that eventually they should no longer be troubled at all by seeing violent images, as a result of desensitisation by systematic repetition. The processes of desensitisation and flooding are well-known methods for modification of behaviour by reducing the impact of the original accompanying emotion.

Because of this knowledge, it has been difficult for psychologists to demonstrate experimentally the effect of images of extreme violence on young children's behaviour. Experiments involving live subjects, and especially young children, would usually be submitted to an ethical committee, who would consider any likely effects. The processes of traumatisation and desensitisation are well enough known for any ethical committee to refuse to sanction the showing of such videos to children in order to monitor effects. Moreover, if it were suggested that parents should watch alongside, child psychologists would be more alarmed still at such a proposal, on the basis that any identification by the child with the violent perpetrator could be additionally enhanced through identification with his parents, were they apparently to accept the film's attitudes.

Thus most research on the results of watching violence either has to follow up long-term effects on individual cases, or has to extrapolate from experimental situations that do not in fact involve witnessing *extreme* violence. Since children's exposure to the kind of sadistic images with which we are now concerned is relatively recent, there has not yet been time to carry out the longitudinal studies that this would involve, while ethical experimental studies are necessarily rather artificial. Nevertheless, Professors Sims and Gray (Professors of Psychiatry and Paediatrics respectively) were able to point to 'a vast world literature, more than 1,000 papers, linking heavy exposure to media violence with subsequent aggressive behaviour' in their document presented to the Broadcasting Group of the House of Lords in September 1993. They made two particularly important points themselves: that in current video material 'unlike traditional gruesome stories, the viewer is made to identify with the *perpetrator* of the act, and not with the victim'; and that:

> watching specific acts of violence on the media has resulted in mimicry by children and adolescents of behaviour that they would otherwise, literally, have found unimaginable.

There is, of course, a connection between identification and mimicry, which decides *what* is mimicked.

George Comstock, Professor of Communications at Syracuse University, New York, reviewed 190 research projects over 30 years on the impact of television violence (remembering the caveats given above); he found 'a very solid relationship between viewing anti-social portrayals or violent episodes and behaving anti-socially' in both boys and girls (Comstock, 1991). Huesmann and Eron at Illinois published a 20-year follow-up of 400 children, and found that heavy exposure to television violence at age eight (again remembering that the violence was by no means as extreme then as now) was associated with violent crime and spouse or child abuse at age 30 – 'at all socio-economic levels and all levels of intelligence....It cannot be denied or explained away'

(Huesmann and Eron, 1986). A British review of 40 adolescent murderers and 200 young sex offenders showed 'repeated viewing of violent and pornographic videos' as 'a significant causal factor'; this was particularly significant in adolescents abusing in babysitting contexts, where videos provided 'a potent source of immediate arousal for the subsequent act', including mimicry of the violent images witnessed (Bailey, 1993).

Implications

There continues to be a need for systematic research in order to keep pace with both the growth of violence in children and the growth of violent visual material available to them. Indeed, the Professor of Psychological Criminology at Cambridge identifies 'a pressing need for a new long-term programme of high-quality Government-funded research on (all) causes of offending' in young people, the cost of which would be 'infinitesimal compared with the costs of almost everything connected with crime' (Farrington, 1994). So far as research on the effect of violent images is concerned, and given the ethical considerations already elaborated, the careful collection of case history material is likely to be the most fruitful. This would, of course, need to be both prospective and retrospective; that is, children's viewing habits (or video knowledge) could be monitored, and eventual outcomes assessed, while child and adolescent offenders could be studied retrospectively in terms of background experience. It is important, of course, to distinguish between offenders against the person and mere offenders against property.

Meanwhile, it seems impossible to allow the situation to continue, and indeed escalate, as it now is. Michael Medved stops short at advocating censorship, and makes a plea for film-makers to set their own standards and limits. Although individuals such as Stanley Kubrick and Anthony Hopkins have begun to have doubts about their own contributions, it seems unlikely that those who feel responsibility for protecting children will be able to wait for such corporate self-denial.

Many of us hold our liberal ideals of freedom of expression dear, but now begin to feel that we were naive in our failure to predict the extent of damaging material and its all too free availability to children. Most of us would prefer to rely on the discretion and responsibility of parents, both in controlling their children's viewing and in giving children clear models of their own distress in witnessing sadistic brutality; however it is unhappily evident that many children cannot rely on their parents in this respect. By restricting such material from home viewing, society must take on a necessary responsibility in protecting children from this as from other forms of child abuse.

(Note that in concentrating here on the needs of children and young people, I have limited myself to my own professional specialism. I do not wish to imply, however, that adults are unaffected by or immune to the destructive influence of images of extreme violence and sadism.)

Postscript

When I wrote this paper, I had no idea how it would be responded to, for the simple reason that there had been very little public discussion of these issues, despite the availability of good research. It was suggested to me that I should test the water by inviting two dozen or so distinguished professionals in child development – psychologists, paediatricians and child psychiatrists – to act as co-signatories if they agreed. I wrote to the first 36 I could think of; 32 wished to support the paper, one agreed but did not want to be named at that time and one felt the matter should be left to parents. I had only known the opinion of three before inviting them, and none of them knew the identity of their co-signatories until much later. I was overwhelmed by the strength of support by both these and the many other people who wrote to me. It was as if suddenly people felt they had the right to speak about long-existing concerns, when previously they had assumed the matter had to be left to media experts.

It was in fact the academics in media studies who criticised most vociferously, and they did indeed take the line that only media specialists had the right to comment, and that child development professionals knew nothing about the media and should keep silent. In this they were markedly different from people actually working in the media, who soon began to produce very thoughtful articles questioning how far it was acceptable for children – or adults, for that matter – to be left entirely unprotected by any kind of regulation. Several women journalists brought to bear their personal experience in trying to protect their own children from sadistic imagery; more difficult for media academics to stomach were articles from distinguished critics and writers such as Martin Amis and Michael Billington, who were known to accept violent imagery and yet were prepared to acknowledge that this could be desensitising and destructive. Billington, for instance, extended the argument to the adult theatre, describing himself as having felt 'diminished and corrupted' by one particular production, and quoted George Steiner:

> if serious literature and the arts can educate sensibility, exalt our perceptions, refine our moral discriminations, they can, by exactly the same token, deprave, cheapen and make bestial our imaginings and mimetic impulses. (Quoted in Billington, 1994)

The criticisms of our concerns have boiled down to perhaps four. Firstly, it was said that in every age there has been a 'moral panic' about the images available to people considered vulnerable, and that concerns about video violence were very like the concerns about penny dreadfuls in the last century. Secondly, it was claimed that films are presented within a moral context in which, although people may get maimed or killed, the baddies get their come-uppance, and therefore the violence is acceptable. Thirdly, it was stated that it had not been proved beyond doubt that violent images beget violent behaviour. Fourthly, there was the argument that the liberty of parents to decide for themselves what their children should see should not be infringed. I would like to say a word about each of these.

The notion of moral panic is a case of arguing by derision; however, I am tempted to remind the deriders of the gloss on Kipling's 'If': 'If you can keep your head when all about you are losing theirs, could be you haven't quite understood the situation'. More seriously, however, the comparison with penny dreadfuls trivialises the issue, and ignores both the seductiveness of colour, movement and sound on film and the added addictiveness and capacity for mimicry that comes with these qualities – which is why advertisers will pay more for a TV advertisement than for a black and white ad in a newspaper.

I have already said something about the somewhat dubious notion that violence is sanitised by being presented as a punishment for people defined as baddies. Even if this were an acceptable argument, there are further observations that have to be set against it. For instance, there is research that shows that young children cannot reliably follow a storyline through a commercial break: this would make it difficult for them to pursue a moral line from the beginning to the end of the story. Add to this that often, in practice, children's attention is *intermittent*: they are not watching for the storyline at all, but just for the punch-up, to which they may contribute with great excitement, lapsing into boredom between bouts. How many of these children understand that morality triumphed rather than fire-power? These critics also make much of the fact that children on the whole know the difference between fact and fantasy; I think they usually do, with some important exceptions, but this does not really seem relevant to the argument.

The question of causal proof carries more weight, and many people will find it abstruse; it includes the notion of consistency. I do not think I can put this better or more succinctly than Dr Catherine Itzin, who discusses it in the related area of pornography and sexual violence, and I therefore quote her:

> Correlation does not prove causality. It never can. Causality is a standard of proof that rarely, if ever, can be achieved, and is barely, if ever, required. However, correlation is itself evidence. Correlation demonstrates a relationship between one thing and another; it establishes a *connection*. Thus, while there is no proof that smoking causes lung cancer (because there are also other variables and factors affecting the health of an individual over a lifetime), the correlation between smoking and lung cancer has been established repeatedly in different research over a long period of time. In the case of smoking, the correlations have been regarded as sufficient evidence to suggest that it is highly likely that a causal link exists between smoking and lung cancer. The medical profession has long been convinced by this evidence, and more recently the Government: only the tobacco industry still argues that there is no proof, and it is motivated by profit to maintain this position. (Itzen, 1991)

The correlations shown between violent images and mimicry of violence are in fact rather stronger and more consistent than those between smoking and cancer.

On the question of parental freedom, (often contrasted with the notion of the nanny state), we would probably all wish parents to enjoy the right to take responsibility for their child's upbringing; however, it is on the question of responsibility that the argument breaks down. Like it or not, there are many parents to whom we are not able to leave the decisions on how to look after their children (while increasing numbers of parents who *are* good at taking decisions feel disempowered in carrying them out). We do not shrink from protecting children from physical and sexual abuse; my concern is that here we have another source of child abuse where children and parents need help for their protection.

Finally, it has sometimes been suggested that expressing concern about the desensitisation of children by brutal images might divert attention from the many inequalities in society that may also contribute. I have to say that I have been calling attention to society's inequalities for the whole of my professional life, starting at a time when it was fashionable to assert that the classless society was already with us. I do not feel it necessary to apologise now for *adding in* a rapidly growing factor which we just might have some chance to control before (as I fear) it is too late.

Aide-Mémoire prepared for House of Commons Home Affairs Committee

Video Violence: Direct Causal Links (to follow evidence given by Professor Elizabeth Newson, 22 June 1994)

Note: The research available is mainly on results of viewing TV violence; violent images available on video tend to be considerably more extreme.

The following are the main references:

- Review of nearly 1,000 studies: (Comstock, 1991). George Comstock holds the Chair of Public Communications (*not* Child Development) at Syracuse University, New York. His review is not confined to American studies. Overall, its main conclusion is that:

  > although some group and cultural distinctions appear, the major finding is that the positive association between...violent entertainment and aggressive behaviour travels well. (Survey data)

  Experimental data on both young children and adolescents leads Comstock to develop a set of 'contingencies', that is a list of very useful guidelines to suggest what *kind* of portrayed violence is especially likely to lead to aggression (pp254–5).

- Review by Ellen Wartella (1995). Professor Sir Michael Rutter chaired the Academia Europaea Study Group on 'Psychosocial disorders in young people', and has kindly let me see the section of their report entitled *Media and Problem Behaviours in Young People*. Wartella refers to:

  > a global international market-place, heavily promoting cultural products saturated with violence, sexuality and commercialism, (into which) young audiences throughout Europe are increasingly drawn

  and also says that it would be 'unreasonable not to examine the heavily American-dominated (research) literature on media effects' as well as the European literature.

  This distinguished study group concluded:

  > Distilling decades of laboratory, survey and field experimental

studies, the current reviews conclude that there is a correlation between violence viewing and aggressive behaviour, a relationship that holds even when a variety of controls are imposed (for example, age of subject, social class, education level, parental behaviour, attitudes towards (aggression), and tends to hold across national boundaries.

- Study of 1,500 12- to 17-year-old males in London (Belson, 1978). This study used very detailed and careful sampling and measurements, with matched respondents. It concluded:

  The evidence gathered through this investigation is very strongly supportive of the hypothesis that high exposure to television violence increases the degree to which boys engage in serious violence. Heavier viewers of television violence commit a great deal more serious violence than do light viewers of television violence who have been matched for a wide array of variables.

- Longitudinal study over 30 years (Huesmann and Eron, 1986). This study is important because the difficulty of separating correlation and causation is much more easily overcome in a longitudinal study. They found that boys' viewing of TV violence at age eight predicted (a) more aggressive behaviour at 18, (b) serious criminal behaviour at age 30. It also predicted harsh punishment of these men's children, thus creating an ongoing spiral of violence. Wartella, reviewing longitudinal studies generally, concludes that 'viewing televised violence leads to aggressive behaviour and not vice versa'. The one US longitudinal study that did not support this (Milavsky and others, 1982) has been very strongly criticised methodologically, and in fact various critics have re-analysed the data to show that it actually supports a causal explanation.

Statements by official bodies

- Select Committee, National Institute of Mental Health, USA, 1982:

  The consensus among most of the research community is that violence on television does lead to aggressive behaviour by children and teenagers who watch the programmes....The research question has moved from asking *whether or not* there is an effect, to seeking *explanations* for the effect.

- The American Psychological Association has put out a similar statement.
- US Attorney General's Commission on Pornography, 1985:

concluded that there were definite links between violent sexually explicit material and harm to women and children.

- Australian Joint Select Committee on Video Material, 1988: concluded pornography was linked to harm.
- Ministerial Committee of Inquiry, New Zealand, 1989: stated that violent, dehumanising and degrading material was harmful to women.
- Study Group Academia Europaea, 1994:

> European insistence that the conclusions from laboratory studies may be dismissed as externally invalid does not address the overall consistency of the survey and field experimental research which...are supportive of a causal link between television violence viewing and aggressive behaviour....Overall these critics [mainly Cumberbatch and Howitt, 1989] do not undermine the substantial body of convincing evidence to show that television violence is among the causes of real-world violence.

Itzin (quoted in my annotations above) and others have pointed out that Dr Cumberbatch's evidence has consistently denied any causal link, has been remarkably at variance with world-wide studies and reviews, and has depended upon assertions that causality cannot be derived from correlation, even in the face of highly consistent correlations which are in fact stronger than those between smoking and cancer. Cumberbatch and his colleagues have been strongly criticised on methodological grounds and for their interpretation of the evidence. In particular, Professor James Check (Director of Research Programme on Violence and Conflict Resolution at York University, Toronto) describes their report to the Home Office (1990) as:

> clearly biased...at best...seen as a polemic for those who wish to promote political views at the expense of scholarship and scientific objectivity.

He writes that Cumberbatch and his colleagues:

> mis-cite, misrepresent and misunderstand a number of studies, either deliberately or through an inability to comprehend the work (particularly when it comes to statistical analyses) and they omit a great deal of the important literature as well as important findings in the studies that they do cite. (Quoted in Itzin, 1991)

The regulation of television viewing within the family

Mark Allerton

Introduction

I want to discuss how families regulate television and video viewing. The question before us is: are electronic children powering ahead or are they a cause for concern? I hope to answer that question by making the case that children and parents are indeed powering ahead, while those working with children all too often only wring their hands in concern. I want to make the case for supporting parents' and children's existing use of positive strategies for regulation, rather than increasing censorship further.

My professional background is as an early years teacher. There is a strong ethos within nursery education that parents are their children's first educators and that it is the job of professionals who work with children to nurture a partnership with parents for the benefit of the child. Such a partnership can be the basis for parents and professionals to learn from each other, and so to enhance children's education. Much has been gained from partnerships like this in reading and maths achievement and in changing parental attitudes towards the long term goals of education.

Nursery education also aims to foster independent thinking skills in children. It aims to help children to make decisions for themselves and to see those decisions through, so that they learn to solve problems on their own. Research from the USA into nursery education, which stresses this kind of independent learning, shows that there are long term benefits in terms of children's adaptation to the adult world. So, as an educationalist, that was my starting point with video and television regulation in families. If we want to change and develop the way television is regulated, we have to work with families in partnership and encourage children to become independent viewers.

To develop these themes, I will refer to a research project funded by the Broadcasting Standards Council between 1993-94. The research grew out of a concern that, in the present era of increasing access to diverse images, the limitations of state censorship are becoming apparent. Wider access means that existing controls are being evaded with ease. Families are in the middle of two competing forces; on the one hand, there is a de-regulated media industry, which encourages children through advertising and peer pressure to watch more and to consume more; and, on the other hand, the censorship lobby which wants to restrict access further, making parents feel guilty and making material attractive to children by giving it the status of forbidden fruit. It seems hypocritical to free the market place and then to condemn the customers for not showing restraint. At the very least, it seems reckless to allow such a free-for-all without giving parents more support than the current classification and watershed systems provide.

With this concern in mind, it seems timely to shift the debate away from the kind of research which tries to establish long term causal effects of television, and to look instead at what children and parents are doing with television. If it can be shown that there are ways in which families are regulating children's viewing effectively under the current system, then the focus of debate should not be on how to further limit access, but on how to develop those efforts for other families and for those who wish to support them.

The Research

We interviewed children and parents at home and at school about regulation. Our interest was in how children regulate themselves, as well as how parents regulate them, so we asked about material that they found to be upsetting on television and video and what they did if they got upset, scared or sad by something that they saw. Seventy-two six- to 16-year-old children from contrasting social areas took part in the research, and 20 sets of their parents. The research was based on group interviews and reveals clear themes which we take to be typical of a range of families' regulatory behaviour. Perhaps just as importantly, we hope that the research will stimulate the debate about regulation in a way which can empower parents and children more effectively than the current system.

The first point that I would like to make about the children we interviewed in this way is that television seems to be a highly emotive stimulus. That is, many different emotions are invoked when children watch television. This is a point worth making at the outset, because there is a common stereotype that children passively absorb images on the screen without reacting and this is not borne out by this research. Our own expectations were also overturned, because we expected the children to talk about being upset mostly by horror films. They actually talked about a wide range of programmes as being upsetting or frightening. Horror films featured prominently but also wildlife documentaries where animals were seen being killed; soap operas in which a favourite character died or left the programme or where there was an abduction; news items about war or about children being hurt or killed (particularly the murder of James Bulger); and anything about families being disrupted.

Children's self-regulation

We defined the children's developing self-regulation as being what they said they did when they got upset, and how they coped with that stress. The theoretical literature on how children cope with stress, such as when undergoing medical procedures or when experiencing bullying at school, proposes that different people cope with the same sort of stresses in different ways according to the meaning that they ascribe to the stressful event (Lazarus and Folkman, 1984). This is similar to how an adult would cope with a horror film on television, which would be to turn to another channel because such images frighten me. According to this theory, then, the meaning that children ascribe to the images they see on television will determine how they cope with any stress it causes.

I would like to illustrate how children cope with being upset or scared with some examples from the research. There is a major difference in how children respond to fiction and non-fiction. Katie (six to seven years) is talking about the children's programme *Animals of Farthing Wood*, a cartoon serial in which a group of animals' habitat is threatened by a road development. (Each remark starts with a number, to help to refer to it in the text.)

> 333   Interviewer: What about you Katie if you've seen something really sad like that is there a way you can change how you feel?

> 334   Katie: Yeah I've already told you stick my head under the pillow so I can't see it.

335   Interviewer: Right so you just sort of take it away then or take yourself away.

336   Katie: Or I put a different film on or I read a book / I normally rush upstairs get a book read it and take my mind off the television [gesture with both hands lifting her mind off] and then read it and I can't...

337   Interviewer: So you do something that will take your mind off it and make you think about something else.

338   Katie: But I don't choose a sad one.

Katie uses distraction to reduce her sadness. Her gesture suggests that the emotion she feels can be put on to one side, her mind can be taken off it (336) and it can be replaced by another emotion, not a sad one but one also produced by fiction. Her accompanying physical gesture, acting out taking her mind away from the sad emotion, is a metaphor for coping which seems very self-aware for a seven-year-old child and suggests that sadness produced by fiction can be substituted by another emotion with ease.

Compare this to the following extract in which two working class girls, Sherrie and Tope, and a boy, Christopher, aged 9 to 10 years, talk about news coverage of Bosnia.

299   Sherrie: And I think that you see people like people who're giving away ten thousand pounds on the telly or something it's stupid because look how the people who really need it in Bosnia and stuff and look how poor they are and they may suffer as well so they shouldn't really be giving / like GMTV every single day for one simple easy little question even I know the question and they're just giving it away and when the Bosnian people come over to this country and they ain't got no one no family over here / that's what happening on the News when I was watching *London Tonight*.

305   Christopher: I know what I would like to do I would feel sad / what was I going to say? // [others talking Interviewer asks them about News] oh yeah I remember what I was going to say / we're lucky we get pounds and 10ps and all that and 20s and 50s for our pocket money when they Bosnia people ain't even got a penny.

307   Interviewer: So if you see something about people in Bosnia you know who haven't got any food or money and that what do you do?

308 Tope: I go to the telly.

309 Interviewer: You go to the telly? What do you do?

310 Tope: I don't know sometimes I hug the telly.

311 Interviewer: You hug it? [laughs] And does that work does that make you feel better?

312 Tope: No.

It can be seen here that Sherrie's knowledge of television helps her to define her emotional response. In her anger at the hypocrisy of giving cash prizes for easy questions when people are suffering in Bosnia (299), she refers to programme types to give her point weight. She compares GMTV's simple, childlike ('even I know the question'), tabloid style with the news programme *London Tonight*. Christopher (305) compares his knowledge of poverty in Bosnia with his own relative wealth, using reflection on his own experience. In referring to his own experience when he says 'we're lucky...', he reinforces the reality of what is happening in Bosnia. The children's coping strategies also reflect a realistic appraisal of their relative powerlessness; Tope hugs the telly but it doesn't help (308–312), Sherrie donates old clothes which does make her feel less sad. These responses are not that different to those many adults experience when faced with images of famine and war – pity, helplessness, anger and charity. We saw this throughout the research, children responding emotionally according to what they perceived a television programme to mean. In this case, the children give clear evidence that what they see happening in Bosnia is a real event, worthy of a sober emotional response. Compared to Katie's response to the cartoon, this response shows that, if children define something as real, their response to the emotions invoked is different.

I now want to show how this kind of self-regulation applies to material which causes more public concern. The children in our research were frightened by what they saw in horror films, but their responses suggested that being frightened was not always unpleasurable or upsetting.

First, I must make a distinction which the children made very clear to us. There is a difference between real fear and pleasurable fear. Real fear may give you nightmares, make you afraid to go up to bed alone or make you afraid to be alone in the house. Pleasurable fear is the thrill of suspense, the thrill of the roller coaster ride and the thrill of being disgusted. The type of fear that you feel when watching depends again on what meaning you ascribe to what you see.

Both real fear and pleasurable fear do elicit coping strategies. The thrill of frightening texts appears to demand suspension of disbelief, making the fear real. Annalisa, Nishith and Natasha (a mixed group of middle class 12- to 13-year-olds) are talking about the horror film *Child's Play 3*, in which a toy doll comes to life and creates mayhem:

> 80   Interviewer: Can you remember a particular scene from it that you found frightening? / I mean you said it was a bit frightening didn't you Annalisa?

> 81   Annalisa: Yeah I hide my eyes at everything though I sit there with my hands over my eyes just peeking out which is really I know it's really stupid 'cos you can still see but I just feel safe 'cos you know how some people they hug a pillow or something well I have to hide my eyes but I still watch it all with my eyes covered and I can remember the bit at the end of *Child's Play 3* when um just when the doll's trying to kill everyone that's always the bits I can remember / killing.

Annalisa's coping strategy here is not intended to remove the frightening image at all but to actually heighten her enjoyment, the thrill of being repelled and attracted at the same time. This ambivalence can be seen in her strategy, she hides her eyes but still watches it all (81). This allows her to feel safe while still being frightened. Her reading of the text as fiction seems to allow her into a state of fear which, while truly frightening and demanding some coping behaviour, is nevertheless pleasurable.

Another way children appraise a text is by using their knowledge of the medium. This kind of knowledge has been described as 'television literacy' (Buckingham, 1993) and involves using a set of skills for reading television in much the same way that the printed word demands specific skills. What we found was that children used different skills according to what it was they were watching, much as a reader reads a newspaper differently to an encyclopaedia. When children defined a film or programme as fictional, their responses were different to when they talked about non-fiction. Within horror films there are different genres which demand different responses from the viewer, for example, the children made a distinction between 'spoof' horror films like *Nightmare On Elm Street* and the *Child's Play* series and more psychological horror films like *Silence of the Lambs*. Josie (13 years) talks about *Nightmare on Elm Street*:

80   Interviewer: What was it about it that frightened you?

81   Josie: I dunno, it wasn't real, like I knew it wouldn't happen in real life it's just like / um the atmosphere 'cos like you think [puts on shivery voice] oh my gosh but, um I dunno really, it was just funny it was funny 'cos you know it wouldn't happen but it was a little bit scary at the same time 'cos you didn't know what was going to happen next.

//

85   Josie: Yeah but it was a bit rubbish, 'cos like they said you can tell 'cos you can tell it wouldn't happen it's just that you didn't know what was going to happen next it wasn't actually the like I thought / you didn't actually think that he existed, like some people do /

Josie talks about the film as an artificial construction of reality, one which is able to frighten her through its use of suspense and atmosphere (81). But her experience was again an ambivalent one, both 'funny' and 'scary'. It is her appraisal of the text as artificial and implausible which frees her to enjoy the thrill of it, rather than having to cope with the real fear of something plausible. Her repeated references to this reality judgement mark her appraisal of the reality status of the film; 'it wasn't real', 'it wouldn't happen in real life', 'it wouldn't happen' (81), 'you can tell it wouldn't happen' and 'you didn't actually think that he existed' (85).

This suggests that children are using their knowledge of and experience of watching television in order to protect themselves. This is the beginning of self-regulation.

The children's judgements about the reality of a programme seemed to be crucial to how much fear it caused. As a case in point, many of the children talked about a programme called *Ghostwatch* which was broadcast on BBC1 at 9.30 p.m. on Saturday, 31 October 1992, Halloween night. This was a fictional programme in which an outside broadcast unit was to spend the night in a haunted house, while in the studio there was a discussion about the paranormal with experts and witnesses and a fictional phone-in for viewers to report their psychic experiences. The haunted house turned out to be very haunted indeed, with objects flying around and mysterious figures appearing. The children we talked to described this programme as the most frightening thing they had ever seen, more frightening than any horror film. Indeed, there was a report in the *British Medical*

Journal that two boys actually experienced post-traumatic stress syndrome after seeing it. The reason that it was so frightening, according to the children in our study, was that they did not know that it was fiction. The programme featured well-known, credible presenters from children's programmes (Sarah Greene and Mike Smith) and was so like the usual format of a documentary investigation that the children's normal protective mechanisms were not available; they felt cheated and very angry that they had been duped. They described watching the programme as a continual struggle to assert whether or not it was really happening and, for most of them, the signs were that it was real and that it was, therefore, very frightening. Other material that children found very frightening because they defined it as real were news items about war or abduction or terrorist attacks or 'real life' dramas involving family disruption or death. Crime reconstructions were also frightening and worrying, especially if they were local and if they involved a child or teenager. In the words of one 13-year-old girl: 'Horror films aren't frightening, what really frightens me is nuclear bombs and the fact that it could really happen.'

Real fear and pleasurable fear elicited very different coping strategies. If the children were enjoying the thrill, then their coping strategy would involve some sort of hiding or avoidance which still enabled them to watch. On the other hand, if they were really scared by something, they would turn to a different channel, turn the set off or decide not to watch similar material in the future.

Examples like this ought not to be taken to mean that if children judge a text to be implausible they will not be scared by it. I do not want to suggest that fiction cannot frighten children. My argument is that whether they are frightened or not, their response will be based on what sense they make of what they see. Children's knowledge of the medium, for example in using the implausibility or artifice of a text to reduce its stressful impact, is just one way in which they appear to do this.

There are many other ways in which children seek to protect or regulate themselves. One 13-year-old boy got particularly upset watching films in which a parent or child dies. He would check with his mother whether a film was likely to feature such a death and then avoid watching it. Younger children talked about seeking physical comfort from an adult if a film became frightening. Children will turn the television off, change channels or turn the sound down. In other situations, children change the viewing context, by switching off a video and watching it at another time when an adult would be around, for instance. In fact, video recorders give children the opportunity to develop coping strategies like this by allowing them to watch something again if they did not understand it fully the first time round, by allowing them to skip over certain sequences and by allowing them to fast forward to see what happens next.

Examples like this ought not to be taken to mean that children who watch a lot of television cannot be frightened by it. There are many examples in the research of younger and older children being very frightened despite their knowledge of the medium. My argument is that, if it can be shown that when children do get frightened they act – they cope in one way or another – this suggests a way in which we can begin to help them above and beyond the existing safeguards. The main source of support for children in developing these coping skills comes from their parents.

Parental regulation

We interviewed 20 of the children's parents in their homes about how they regulated television. These 20 were by no means representative of the general population; all 72 were invited to take part and we interviewed 20 who formed a mix of families from different social class and cultural backgrounds, with children of different ages and several single parent families. What I shall talk about is not meant to be a survey of how much television parents let their children watch across the country, but a snapshot of these 20 families. The strategies these parents use can be seen as the basis for providing the kind of support that I believe families want.

The first thing to say about parental regulation is that the children's age makes a great difference. The parents we interviewed all acknowledged that their control had decreased as their children got older. By interviewing the parents of older and younger children we were able to build up a cross-sectional picture of how the process of regulation changed with age. We found that up to the age of about eight to nine years most children's viewing was quite carefully and effectively regulated. With young children, the parents found it relatively easy to control what they watched by invoking bedtime, or by using the children's own ignorance of when films that might become the focus of dispute were to be shown. In these cases, the parents' control was absolute – if they didn't think their children should watch something they just said no.

As children got older and more external concerns crept into their lives, like homework, more negotiation took place about what they were allowed to watch. All the parents used homework as a way of limiting viewing, although the number of children with televisions in their own rooms made this more difficult. The parents, on the whole, dealt with this problem by being quite firm to begin with over televisions being on while the children worked, but recognising as the children got older that a certain amount of trust and independent decision making had to be allowed if they were not to be continually checking. One family deeply regretted allowing their teenage children to have televisions, not because they were worried about them watching unsuitable material, but because it meant that the amount of social interaction within the family was greatly reduced.

As children got into adolescence, homework and banning of programmes gave way to negotiation. The parents we interviewed had a range of sensible strategies to help them through this difficult period. Some parents previewed a film themselves before deciding whether their children could watch it. This is one of the great advantages of video technology for regulation: programmes or films can be taped and watched by parents first. Material which parents are not sure about or they would like to watch alongside their children can be taped and watched together. Something which is potentially upsetting can be watched at a time when a parent can be on hand to explain and talk about the subject matter.

All of these strategies reflected one overwhelming concern about television and video for this group of parents. What concerned these parents was that their children might be upset by things that they saw; that their children might get nightmares or be unable to understand what they had seen. They were emphatically not worried about the long term effects of television on their children. They were also not worried about their children imitating violence. Some parents acknowledged that their children did copy martial arts moves, for instance, from the television, but they denied that this would make their children more violent. Parents seemed to use the same sort of judgements as the children we interviewed regarding material which was generally seen as unrealistic or fantasy violence, such as the *Terminator* films, and these type of films were not something that most parents chose to ban after their children reached eight or nine years of age.

The parents' dilemma seemed to be that they did not want their children to be upset, frightened or worried by what they saw, but they also wanted to allow their children to learn to make their own decisions, especially as they got older. There was a recognition that children needed to be protected, but that it was also in their interest not to be sheltered too much. The parents also accepted that it was inevitable that their children would see things they did not approve of elsewhere and preferred to prepare them for that in their own home. In the words of one Asian father:

> 'I think I pride myself with my kids that I do not frighten them. I will try and explain if they are frightened of anything. I will explain to them why it's frightening and what takes place and what's the reason for it. Because I've seen a lot of kids that won't go in the dark because they're scared....I like my kids to be independent and confident, so I will explain and reassure them that it does not happen, so don't be afraid....Again I think it goes back to when I was growing up and I think I watched *Quatermass* when I was about eight...I watched it in black and white and my dad was quite strict and they all went to bed and I crept down and watched *Quatermass* and I thought it was absolutely frightening but I had nobody to tell me that it's not true.'

The parents recognised that when the children were young they needed a protective atmosphere which, through the teenage years, needed to be allowed slowly to decrease and independence allowed to grow. One set of parents taped *The Lion, the Witch and the Wardrobe* a week in advance, so that when their six- and seven-year-old children saw the penultimate episode in which the lion was killed, they already had the final episode to hand where the lion comes back to life. These parents were anticipating their children's level of upset and providing protection by avoiding an agonising week long wait to see if the lion really was dead. The father who watched the film *The Doors*, so that he knew what it was his 14-year-old son wanted to watch and could talk to him about drug and alcohol abuse, accepted that his son was going to watch the film, but also knew that some measure of protection and support may be necessary.

One final point before I conclude. In discussing their children's responses to television, parents frequently stressed differences between their children. They would say that they would let one child watch something which another, perhaps older child, would not be allowed to. This knowledge of their own children had been built up over the years by making mistakes in allowing them to watch certain programmes which they did not expect the children to find frightening, or preventing them from watching things which, in the end, did not bother them. This well of knowledge was what most of the parents said formed their yardstick for regulation – in the end, it was a matter of knowing your children and not something that could be reduced to a set of age limits.

I am aware that I have dwelled on the negative side of television regulation, since that is what causes most concern. But there is a positive side to regulation, which many parents illustrated in our research. There were parents who used television as an aid to educate their children, one family had watched the film *JFK* and the children had followed up their interest by getting books about Kennedy from the library. There were parents who used the issues brought up in soap operas to give their own view so that their children heard a balance of views about, for instance, domestic violence. There were parents who recognised the power of television to educate children about the natural world and encouraged their children to watch wildlife documentaries. This kind of positive experience, where children are encouraged to watch in order to educate and extend their experiences, is as much a part of regulation as restricting access in order to protect children from being too upset.

Finally, the parents in our study all talked about using the existing system of classification and the watershed as broadly useful guidelines. They also recognised that the existing legislation represents the limit that external regulation can reach. They saw themselves as being in the front line of regulation and used their own discretion and knowledge of their own children far more than age classifications or the watershed.

Conclusions ᘮ woll

First, if children use their knowledge of television in order to regulate themselves, then one obvious conclusion is that school curricula should help them to develop the skills necessary to do this. Media education from an early age would help children not only to demystify what they see on screen but also to reflect on what they have seen and how it relates to their personal experience.

Second, forewarned is forearmed; parents need more information about individual programmes and films than they are currently given. This would enable them to better predict how their children may react and to help them to decide how to regulate a particular film or programme. Whether, for example, it is the kind of film that they feel they can let their children watch alone or whether they feel they should watch it alongside them. Television listings magazines could do this with ease and the retail video industry should be able to provide accessible information through monthly bulletins.

Third, there is a need for programme-makers to be sensitive to the methods that children use to make sense of their programmes. Programmes which children perceive to be real are potentially upsetting. *Ghostwatch* is a case in point, but news items are seen as real by children and should be scheduled sensitively so that parents can be aware of what their children could be watching. Breakfast news, in particular, has been guilty of forgetting that children could be watching.

Fourth, I am aware that the picture of parenting which emerges from our research may seem particularly rosy. Our sample was not representative and I do not deny that there may be parents who do not regulate viewing as I have described. But if we are to find a way forward to support families, what better model of regulation than that offered by these parents?

So, finally, there is a need for parental education which can develop the strategies we have identified and make them available to a wide range of parents. There are obvious outlets for publicising this kind of work, like schools, clinics and health services. But the most effective medium would be television itself and I believe it is time that television companies come forward and invest in supporting families' already extensive efforts at regulating children's television viewing.

Part 2: Playing games with computers

Introduction

Tim Gill

Computer games are one of the marketing phenomena of the 1990s. By 1993, 60 per cent of children owned a computer games machine and 80 per cent played regularly (figures quoted in Cunningham, 1995). The decrease in sales since then may have more to do with market saturation than any drop in interest.

There are strong similarities between television watching and computer game use, viewed as children's leisure activities. Both are sedentary, take place indoors, and engage children through screen images and sounds. However, there are perhaps three important differences between the two electronic media. First, computer games actively involve children; the games demand choices, develop certain kinds of skill, foster competition (and sometimes cooperation) between players and in some cases encourage tactical and strategic awareness. Second, almost all games are explicitly aimed at children; by comparison, while there are child-oriented television programmes and videos, children themselves tend to prefer adult programmes (Bazalgette and Buckingham, 1995), so the medium as a whole cannot be said to be aimed at children. Finally, games are more expensive than either videos or television; compare the cost of games software with that of video purchase or rental. Apart from anything else, this means that parents can exert greater control over their children's choices (in theory at least).

So one might conclude that computer games have a lot to offer, both to children looking for an engaging challenge, and to parents searching for safe ways for their children to spend their leisure time. But many adults have reached very different conclusions. Parental fears about 'addiction', health consequences and the effects of violent or stereotyped content clearly resonate with the image of an electronic Pied Piper. Mark Griffiths' paper, which summarises research into the consequences of computer game use, questions the significance of these fears. His own statistic for heavy games use (around seven per cent of children say they play for 30 hours per week or more), while perhaps not entirely reassuring, is hardly the stuff of moral panics. As Libby Purves argues in her contribution, one needs to keep a sense of proportion. To take another example, newer research from Griffiths and his colleagues found that about a quarter of children reported neglecting homework to play (Phillips and others, 1995), a finding greeted with headlines in some of the broadsheets. Yet we all know that it does not take too much to tempt schoolchildren away from homework. Indeed this forces us to ask if there is anything about computer game 'addiction' that makes it so different to any other leisure activity that periodically engulfs some children's lives: activities like football, chess, keeping pets, skateboarding or pog (a game that swept through school playgrounds in 1995, and involves nothing more high-tech than a stack of small plastic or cardboard discs).

Griffiths also points out that many of the games available contain little or no violent imagery. Victor John, a 14-year-old pupil at Graveney School, prefers to play the car racing games and flight simulators. 'I find them most challenging as you have to solve different problems', he says. His fellow pupil, Shem Pennant, also points out that 'not all computer games are violent. I personally prefer adventure games...I like strategy games that tax the mind.'

Computer games undeniably draw on stereotyped images of gender, as many researchers have shown (see for instance Provenzo, 1991). Moreover, these stereotyped protrayals of male and female characteristics go some way to explaining why game playing is more popular with boys than girls, as Griffiths suggests. Not surprisingly, girl pupils from Graveney School confirm Griffiths' findings on gender differences: 'I dislike computer games and also think that games can be bad for you', says Natasha Mudhar, while Debbie Lovell feels that games are 'all just fighting and shooting, and I'm sure that's the only reason my brother uses them.' But this is not to say that girls do not play computer games, or enjoy them (see for instance Cunningham, 1995). In commercial terms, gender bias can probably be easily explained; with computers, as with children's television, the manufacturers' guiding principle is 'when in doubt, use boys' (Schneider, 1987).

Elizabeth Stutz explores in some depth the issue of gender stereotyping in her paper. A long-standing advocate of the benefits of play, Stutz starts her paper with an overview of children's play: what it means for children and what it gives to children. She argues that electronic entertainment constrains, even destroys, children's play experiences. 'Children are bored', she writes, 'and no longer know how to occupy themselves.' However, she hopes that games manufacturers will develop new kinds of games, as well as arguing for the need to provide 'a pleasing and inviting environment near children's homes'.

Computer game playing in children and adolescents: A review of the literature

Mark Griffiths

Since the introduction of Pong, a computerised table tennis game in 1972, the computer game industry has become big business (Kerr, 1982). Pong led to a substantial increase in the home video game market. However, it was not until the advent of the arcade game Space Invaders in 1979 that video games became popular to a mass audience. By 1981, no single game dominated the field as games like Galaxian, Pac-man and Donkey Kong rendered Space Invaders obsolete (Surrey, 1982).

At present, electronic games can be delivered via four general hardware systems including handheld, personal computer, home video console and arcade machines (Nawrocki and Winner, 1983). Most research on the effects of electronic gaming has centred upon the playing of arcade video games and the alleged negative consequences, that is 'video game addiction' (Soper and Miller, 1983). Little research has been carried out into non-arcade electronic game playing as it has traditionally been perceived as a harmless and enjoyable activity. However, a recent explosion in the UK home computer game market has fuelled press speculation that some children are becoming 'keyboard junkies' (Neustatter, 1991). In 1991, UK sales of console games connected to the television set grew by 200 per cent and sales of handheld games rose by 700 per cent (Economist Intelligence Unit, 1991). The Economist Intelligence Unit predicts that by 1995, one in four boys will own a handheld game. The current debate is whether home or handheld computer games stimulate scientific interests or just turn children into mindless computer game addicts.

A market research survey on attitudes towards computer games (Microprose, 1992) revealed that of the 860 male only respondents (aged 15 years and upwards) only 26 per cent thought they were of educational value although 60 per cent felt the games did not have any disruptive influence on family life. In the 15- to 24-year-old age group, 23 per cent thought that computer games were addictive, 20 per cent thought they were distracting and only 17 per cent thought they were educational. Commenting on these results, Paul Moodie, the managing director of Microprose said,

> much has been written recently about the detrimental effects of computer games, not least of which is that it interferes with children's education. This really couldn't be further from the truth, as recent studies show that computer game users have a higher than average IQ and that game play contributes to computer literacy. Some very emotive words – like addiction – are being tagged to game use when in fact [our games] produce enquiry, investigation and logical thinking. (Microprose, 1992, p2)

It is difficult to see how Moodie reached these conclusions based on the results of his own company's market research, although easy to understand when taking account of his vested interest. This paper therefore attempts to put this debate into an empirical perspective by reviewing the sparse psychological literature on non-arcade computer games and supplementing it with potentially relevant literature from the research into the psychological effects of excessive television watching and excessive arcade video game playing.

Demographic variables

To date there have been few systematic studies on the demographics of computer game playing outside of the video arcade. Those surveys which have reported on the incidence of video arcade playing have concluded that they are mostly played by adolescents with approximately nine out of ten teenagers in the US playing them at some time in their teenage years (Atari, 1982; Gallup, 1982). Incidence figures in the UK are lower but the games are still predominantly played by adolescents (Roberts and Pool, 1988; Graham, 1988). Home computer playing is not demographically different to arcade game playing as most of the limited empirical evidence suggests computer game playing is a youth phenomenon. One slight difference is that home computer game players are younger than the average arcade video player (Griffiths and Hunt, 1993; 1995).

The significant association between gender and frequency of electronic game playing has often been reported (Kaplan, 1983; Griffiths, 1991a). However, reasons as to why males play electronic games significantly more than females have been generally lacking. One explanation may be the content of the games. Braun and others (1986) reported that in 21 games they examined, 12 contained exclusively masculine images, two contained both masculine and feminine images, seven contained neither and none contained exclusively female images. Another explanation may be that of socialisation. Women have not been encouraged to express aggression in public and are unlikely to feel comfortable with games of combat or war (Surrey, 1982). This explanation was partly supported by Morlock, Yando and Nigolean (1985) in a study of 117 undergraduate video game players. Males reported that they play to master the games and for competition whereas females preferred more whimsical, less aggressive and less demanding games than males.

Another factor which may be important in explaining sex differences is that males on average perform better in visual and spacial skills – particularly depth perception and image solving (Maccoby and Jacklin, 1974). These skills are essential in good game playing since good hand–eye coordination is needed in addition to the quick judgements of spacial relationships (Kiesler, Sproull and Eccles, 1983). Kiesler and his colleagues noted that since boys would tend to score higher than girls due to the differences in visual and spacial skills, the girls' average lower scores could be considered a discouraging factor in their reluctance to playing video games.

Video games have the capability to bypass the problems of gender identification (Cooper and Mackie, 1986) and yet most manufacturers choose not to. Gutman (1982) pointed out that on the whole, computer game software is designed by males for males. Some manufacturers realised there was a potential market for females and introduced software she-versions of popular male dominated games such as Ms Pac-man (although all that was changed was the sex of the character, not the content of the game). With regards to hardware, Nintendo recently made an attempt to introduce a Game Girl (a companion to the Game Boy) into the Japanese market but was unsuccessful. Anecdotal evidence suggests that video arcades, even with the introduction of she-versions of popular games, have remained a predominantly male outlet where girls go along in a 'cheerleader' role to admire their boyfriend's playing ability (Griffiths, 1991b). There is at present little evidence to suggest this is the case with non-arcade computer games although the games company Microprose have been reported as having a 98 per cent male clientele (Homer, 1992). It could be that male domination of arcade video games is due more to the arcade atmosphere, its social rules and socialisation factors than the games themselves.

Positive benefits

There are many authors who ardently support the use of computer games, most of whom do so for educational reasons. Silvern (1986) noted that some children may only be drawn into learning through fun and has therefore argued that classroom computer games would be of educational use. Loftus and Loftus (1983) have advocated three ways in which computer games could be put to educational use. They propose that:

● there should be specifically designed games to run on computers already in school;
● educational games should be marketed for the home computer;
● arcade video games should be modified to include educational features.

Similar recommendations have also been put forward by Chaffin, Maxwell and Thompson (1982). Hubbard (1991) reported that computer games had now become an integral part of modern language teaching in the US because they were seen:

> as a motivating device, a means for providing comprehensible input and a catalyst for communicative practice and the negotiation of meaning. (p220)

However, Hubbard went on to say that whether a game is perceived as educational depended on a number of factors including age, gender, proficiency level and cultural background.

In a pioneering study on the use of computer games in education, Malone (1981) concluded that three primary factors in intrinsic motivation for electronic game play were challenge, curiosity and fantasy. The use of these components in the design of a computer game could not only make the games more fun, but also more educational. Sutton-Smith (cited in Surrey, 1982) argues that video games are a good influence because they give children access to 'state of the art' technology. It has also been similarly argued by Gordon (also cited in Surrey, 1982) that electronic games give children a sense of confidence and equip them with computer related skills for the future, although there was no mention of what exactly these skills were.

Brown (1989) has argued that electronic gaming is an exercise in fantasy and that this can have an important effect on outcomes in reality. According to Brown, these biological functions include:

- the regulation of arousal (a decrease through escape or recreation or an increase through competition);
- the preparation for reality (in that some games protect individuals from the full consequences of new perspectives via simulation); and
- the regulation of confidence (in that winning is ego boosting and anxiety reducing which can materially affect other decisions).

It must be noted that Brown's assertions were based on intuition rather than empirical evidence, although his 'preparation for reality' function (simulation) is used by organisations such as the armed forces, who use computer games in the testing of skilled motor performance (Nawrocki and Winner, 1983). The Performance Evaluation Tests for Environmental Research project has already demonstrated that some electronic games are reliable and valid measures of psychomotor skills (Carter, Kennedy and Bittner, 1980; Jones, 1981) and that the US Army use games to train gunners (Trachtman, 1981). It has also been reported that US Navy officials frequent video arcades to recruit trainees with the promise that the US Navy has a greater selection and better quality games on offer! (Soper and Miller, 1983).

Supporters of computer games also argue that they promote social interaction and growth (Favaro, 1982). In a study of the impact of home computer games on family life, Mitchell (1985) reported that families generally felt computer games promoted family interaction in a beneficial way through cooperation and competition. Creasey and Myers (1986) assessed the impact of home computer games on children's leisure activities, school work and peer contacts. Since none of these activities was affected, Creasey and Myers concluded that owning a home video game machine does not have any detrimental effects. With regards to the debate on computer game violence and aggression, some authors have argued that the aggressive content of computer games, rather than having a negative effect, allows the players to release their stress and aggression in a non-destructive way and has the effect of relaxing the players (Bowman and Rotter, 1983; Kestenbaum and Weinstein, 1985), although there is little empirical support for such assertions. Further positive and/or therapeutic effects cited in the literature have included increased hand–eye coordination, attention span and motivation

(Butterfield, 1983), the enhancement of cognitive skills (Green-field, 1983), a sense of mastery, control and accomplishment (Anderson and Ford, 1986) and a reduction in other youth problems due to the 'addictive interest' in video games (Anderson and Ford, 1986)! It is clear from the summary in this section that there appear to be some genuine applied aspects of computer game playing. However, it must be noted that many of the assertions outlined were subjectively formulated and not based on empirical research findings.

The therapeutic value of computer games

Therapists working with children have long used games in therapy and games for therapy in sessions with their young patients (Gardner, 1991). Play has been a feature in therapy since the work of Anna Freud (1928) and Melanie Klein (1932) and has been used to promote fantasy expression and the ventilation of feeling. The recent technological explosion has brought a proliferation of new games which some therapists claim to be an excellent ice-breaker and rapport builder with children in therapy and behaviour management (Spence, 1988; Gardner, 1991). Research in the mid-1980s had already suggested that computer games may actually facilitate cooperative behaviour and reinforcement in more educational settings (Strein and Kochman, 1984; Salend and Santora, 1985).

Gardner (1991) claimed that the use of computer games in his psychotherapy sessions provided common ground between himself and his client and provided excellent behavioural observation opportunities. According to Gardner such observations allowed him to observe:

- the child's repertoire of problem solving strategies;
- the child's ability to perceive and recall subtle cues as well as foresee consequences of behaviour and act on past consequences;
- eye–hand coordination;
- the release of aggression and control;
- the ability to deal with appropriate methods of dealing with the joys of victory and frustrations of defeat in a more sports oriented arena;
- the satisfaction of cognitive activity in the involvement of the recall of bits of basic information;
- the enjoyment of mutually coordinating one's activities with another in the spirit of cooperation.

Gardner went on to describe four particular case studies where computer games were used to support psychotherapy and added that although other techniques were used as an adjunct in therapy (such as storytelling, drawing or other games), it was the computer games that were the most useful factors in the improvement during therapy. It is Gardner's contention that one's clinical techniques tend to change as a function of the trends of the times, though one's goals remain the same. Slower paced and more traditional activities like those outlined above may lengthen the time it takes to form a therapeutic relationship as the child may perceive the therapist not to be 'cool' or 'with it'.

Spence (1988) is another advocate of the therapeutic value of computer games and has incorporated them into his repertoire of behaviour management techniques. Spence believes that computer games can be used instrumentally to bring about changes in a number of areas, and has provided case study examples for each of these changes. These are briefly outlined below:

- Development of relationships: subject used computer games to provide the basis to develop a therapeutic relationship. The computer games gave an acceptable 'middle' ground for both parties to 'meet' which provided an enjoyable experience which could be shared. Relationships become close and trusting.

- Motivation: subjects used computer games as bargaining 'counters' to motivate children to do things. This simply involved negotiating with an individual for a set period of work time or tasks in return for a set period of time playing computer games.

- Cooperative behaviour: subjects used computer games to develop social skills and cooperation in individuals by making them share a computer with peers. Through the medium of computer games, individuals developed friendships which fostered cooperation.

- Aggressive behaviour: subjects used computer games to take the 'heat' out of situations; individuals played computer games when they were angry so that the 'damage' was inflicted on the computer games' characters rather than human beings.

- Self-esteem: subjects used computer games as a measure of achievement to raise self-esteem. Since computer games are skill based and provide scores, they can be compared and provide a basis for future goals. Beating personal high scores raised self-esteem in the individual.

As can be seen from Spence's brief summaries, the benefits outlined are similar to those outlined by Gardner (1991).

There have also been a number of innovative uses of computer games in other therapeutic contexts (Leerhsen, Zabarsky and McDonald, 1983). For instance, 'video game therapy' has been used by Lynch (1981; 1983) for various types of mental disorders, such as stroke patients. Not only can computer game performance be compared between patients and 'normals', but computer game playing can be used as a training aid to some cognitive and perceptual–motor disorders. Further to this, Szer (1983) reported the case of using video game playing as physiotherapy for someone with an arm injury and Phillips (1991) reported the case of using a handheld video game (Nintendo Game Boy) to stop an eight-year-old boy picking at his face. In this latter case, the child had neurodermatitis and scarring due to continual picking at his upper lip. Previous treatments had included a brief behaviour modification programme with food rewards for periods free of picking and the application of a bitter tasting product to the child's fingers. These failed to work so Phillips recommended the use of a handheld computer game, a psychologically rewarding experience that kept the boy's hands occupied. After two weeks the affected area had healed and at a two month follow up, Phillips reported no problems related to the child's continued use of the game. Phillips also reported that video games had been used as a diversion from the side effects of cancer chemotherapy during childhood.

Negative effects: aggression

'Are computer games detrimental to a young person's healthy development?' is the question at the centre of almost all debate concerning the playing of computer games. One of the main concerns that has constantly been raised is that most games feature some kind of aggressive metaphor, and this has led some people to state (without empirical evidence) that children become more aggressive after playing such games (Koop, 1982; Zimbardo, 1982).

There has been a much reported (and debated) link between television violence and violence in children's behaviour (such as Berkowicz, 1970; Andison, 1977; Eron, 1982). With this debate in mind, Silvern, Williamson and Countermine (1983) noted there were similarities between television and video games in that both of these media have entertainment value, violent content and physical feature similarities (such as action, pace and visual change). However, the similarity between violent television and computer game content may be culturally specific, and bearing this in mind, perhaps should not be adopted uncritically into a UK context.

Many authors claim that most computer games are violent in nature and feature death and destruction (Dominick, 1984; Loftus and Loftus, 1983). In a survey reported by Bowman and Rotter (1983), 85 per cent of games that were examined (n=28) involved participants in acts of simulated destruction, killing or violence. A more recent study of computer game content by Provenzo (1991) reported that of the 47 leading Nintendo games that he analysed, only seven of them did not involve violence. He reported that computer games were populated by characters like terrorists, prizefighters, SWAT teams and robotic cops, and that women were cast as 'victims' and foreigners as 'baddies'. Findings such as this led Provenzo to conclude that computer games encourage sexism, violence and racism by conditioning children to view the world in the way that they see on the computer screen.

Although the analyses of computer game content have led researchers to conclude that most computer games are violent, their choice of games for analysis does not necessarily coincide with those games which are the best selling. By looking at any of the 'top ten games' charts in the mass of monthly computer game magazines, it can be seen that many of the most popular games are definitely not 'violent' (examples include Super Mario, in which the actor jumps on mushrooms and turtles killing neither, Sonic the Hedgehog, in which the actor jumps on shapes and spiky creatures to reveal cute animals, and Pacmania in which the actor eats dots or spots).

At present little is known about the long term effects of playing violent computer games but great concern has been raised that computer games may have a greater adverse effect on children than television because of the child's active involvement. Television is only a passive, one way communicative medium (Bowman and Rotter, 1983). Greenfield (1984) has further pointed out that children prefer games over television because there is greater control.

Research into the effects of violent computer games is steadily growing. There are at present only a handful of published studies examining the possible 'aggression' link between games and children's subsequent behaviour and these have only examined the short term effects. These studies were reviewed by Griffiths

(1991a) who concluded that a majority of the studies – especially on very young children as opposed to those in their teenage years – tended to show that children do become more aggressive after either playing or watching a violent game. However, there was much speculation as to whether the procedures used to measure aggression levels were valid and reliable measures. There are also problems concerning the definition of 'violent'. Television cartoons such as *Road Runner* and *Tom and Jerry* are highly violent in nature, but may not be regarded as violent within the operational definitions employed in mass media research. Since almost all computer games are animated, the same argument might be used for them also. Evaluation of the available evidence would seem to suggest that the effects of long term exposure to computer games on subsequent aggressive behaviour remains at best speculative.

Negative effects: physical and social consequences

The medical profession has also voiced a number of concerns about computer game playing. According to Loftus and Loftus (1983), new kinds of pain have been reported. Rheumatologists have described cases of 'Pac-man's Elbow' and 'Space Invaders' Revenge' in which players have suffered skin, joint and muscle problems from repeated button hitting and joystick pushing on the game machines. In a survey by Loftus and Loftus, 65 per cent of (arcade) computer game players examined (n=142) complained of blisters, calluses, sore tendons, and numbness of fingers, hands and elbows directly as a result of their playing. There have also been a number of case studies which have reported some of the adverse effects of playing (non-arcade) computer games. These have included wrist pain (McCowan, 1981), neck pain (Miller, 1991), elbow pain (Bright and Bringhurst, 1992), tenosynovitis (also called 'nintendinitis') (Reinstein, 1983; Brasington, 1990; Casanova and Casanova, 1991; Siegal, 1991), peripheral neuropathy (Friedland and St John, 1984), enuresis (Schink, 1991), encoprisis (Corkery, 1990) and epileptic seizures (Rushton, 1981; Dahlquist, Mellinger and Klass, 1983; Hart, 1990). Admittedly some of these adverse effects are quite rare and 'treatment' simply involved non-playing of the games in question. In the cases involving enuresis and encoprisis, the children were so engaged in the games that they did not want to go to the toilet. In these cases they were simply taught how to use the game's 'pause' button.

Other speculative (but not empirically tested) negative

aspects of computer game playing that have been reported include the belief that computer game play is socially isolating and prevents children from developing social skills (Zimbardo, 1982). For instance, Selnow (1984) reported that video game players use the machine as an 'electronic friend'. This assertion has been tested experimentally by Scheibe and Erwin (1979) who studied the conversations of people with video games while they were playing them. Out of 40 subjects, spontaneous ver-balisations were frequent and recorded in 39 cases, averaging one comment every 40 seconds. They reported the widespread use of pronouns for the machine: 'it hates me', 'he's trying to get me' or 'you dumb machine', but interestingly no use of the pro-noun 'she'. The remarks themselves fell into two categories – direct comments to the machine and simple exclamations or expletives. Scheibe and Erwin concluded that players were reacting to video game machines as if they were people. Similar results have also been obtained by Griffiths (1994) in his analy-sis of fruit machine players. However, this does not necessarily mean that players play the machines instead of forming human friendships and interacting with their peer groups. It has also been suggested that computer game playing may prevent chil-dren and adolescents from participating in more educational pursuits (Egli and Meyers, 1984). However, the very large num-ber of magazines available to game players suggests that those who play a lot may also read a lot. This may further suggest that the threat of an educational deficit (or at least a reading deficit) may not be as great as often imagined, although a more system-atic follow up would be needed to confirm such a claim.

Negative effects: addiction

The most popular argument against computer playing is that it is potentially addictive (Anderson and Ford, 1986). According to Soper and Miller (1983) 'video game addiction' (which is generi-cally similar if not identical to computer game addiction) is like any other behavioural addiction and consists of a compulsive behavioural involvement, a lack of interest in other activities, association mainly with other addicts, and physical and mental symptoms when attempting to stop the behaviour (such as 'the shakes'). Anecdotal and journalistic accounts of computer game addicts ('keyboard junkies') have become increasingly popular in the press. Computer game addiction has rarely been empirically studied, most probably because people feel the area to be trivial and unworthy of academic research. One way of determining whether computer game addiction is addictive in a non-meta-phorical sense is to compare it against clinical criteria for other addictions. This method of making behavioural excesses more clinically identifiable has recently been proposed for 'television addiction' (McIlwraith and others, 1991) and 'amusement machine addiction' (Griffiths, 1991a; 1992). The lack of either operational definitions or diagnostic criteria for computer game addiction probably accounts for the dearth of 'hard data' concerning its existence.

Shotton (1989) carried out a UK study specifically on computer game addiction using a sample of 127 people (half being children, half adult; 96 per cent male) who had been self reportedly 'hooked' on home computer games for at least five years. Seventy-five of these were measured against two control groups and it was reported that the computer dependent individuals were highly intelligent, motivated and achieving people but often misunderstood. After a five year follow up, Shotton found that the younger cohort had done well educationally, gone on to university and then into high ranking jobs. However, Shotton's research was done with people who were familiar with the older generation of computer games which were popular in the earlier part of the 1980s. The computer games of the 1990s may in some way be more psychologically rewarding than the games of a decade ago in that they require more complex skills and improved dexterity as well as having socially relevant topics and better graphics. Anecdotal accounts of greater psychological rewards could mean that the newer games are more 'addiction inducing', although such an assertion needs empirical backing.

If computer games are addictive, what is the addictive process? One potential way of answering this question is to produce possible theoretical accounts of computer addiction and test the hypotheses empirically. McIlwraith (1990) proposed four theoretical models of television addiction in the popular and psychological literature which would seem good models to test the boundaries of computer game addiction. Substituting 'computer game' for 'television' in McIlwraith's account would leave the four explanations as these:

- Computer game addiction is a function of the computer game's effects on imagination and fantasy life: people who play computer games to excess have poor imaginations.
- Computer game addiction is a function of the computer game's effects on arousal level: people who play computer

games to excess either do so for its arousing or tranquillising effects.

- Computer game addiction is a manifestation of oral, dependent or addictive personality: people who play computer games to excess do so due to their inner personality as opposed to the external source of the addiction.
- Computer game addiction is a distinct pattern of uses and gratifications associated with the computer game medium: people who play computer games to excess enjoy the physical act of playing or play only when they are bored.

None of these explanations for computer games have been empirically studied, although anecdotal evidence and evidence from arcade video addiction appears to support the second theoretical orientation. Griffiths (1991b; 1991c) has reported the existence of at least two types of amusement machine addict. The first type appears to be addicted to the machine itself (a 'primary addiction') and plays to test their skill, to get social rewards and most of all for excitement (that is, played for its arousing properties). The second type appears to play machines as a form of escapism, where the machine is possibly an 'electronic friend', played for its tranquillising properties. These players are usually depressed, socially isolated and are those who fit the 'lone addict' media image. This is what could be termed a 'secondary addiction' in that the player uses the machines to escape the primary problem (perhaps a broken home, physical disability or relationship break up). If the primary problem is resolved the excessive machine playing disappears. (Two such case studies involving fruit machine addicts have recently been reported by Griffiths, 1991d). Such a distinction has obvious clinical usefulness.

More recently, there are further reports of behavioural signs of video and computer game dependency. These have included stealing money to play arcade games (Klein, 1984; Keepers, 1990), stealing money to buy new games cartridges (Griffiths and Hunt, 1993), engaging in minor delinquent acts (Kestenbaum and Weinstein, 1985), using lunch money to play (McClure and Mears, 1984), truanting from school (Keepers, 1990; Griffiths and Hunt, 1993), not doing homework/getting bad marks at school (Griffiths and Hunt, 1993), sacrificing social activities (Egli and Meyers, 1984; Griffiths and Hunt, 1993) and an increase in self reported levels of aggression (Griffiths and Hunt, 1993). There is no doubt that for a minority of children and adolescents, video and computer games can take up considerable time and that to all intents and purposes they are addicted to them. However, the prevalence of such an addiction amongst the adolescent community is still of great controversy.

This is one area where research appears to be much needed. The need to establish the incidence and prevalence of clinically significant problems associated with computer game addiction is of paramount importance. As was mentioned at the beginning of this section, clearer operational definitions are required if this is to be achieved.

Treatment of computer game addiction

In addition to the concept of 'computer game addiction', there is also the associated problem of treating 'computer game addicts'. To date, most recommendations have been based on common sense generalisations from self control over other habits, with very few empirical accounts of the treatment of computer game addiction. Kuczmierczyk, Walley and Calhoun (1987) reported the case of an 18-year-old college student who had been playing video games three to four hours a day at an average cost of five dollars a day over a five month period. Kuczmierczyk and his colleagues assumed that compulsive video game playing was conceptually similar to pathological gambling and used a cognitive-behavioural modification approach in their treatment. Using a combination of self-monitoring, GSR (galvanic skin response) biofeedback assisted relaxation training, in vivo exposure and response prevention, a 90 per cent reduction of playing was observed, and confirmed at six and 12 month follow ups. In addition, the patient reported a more satisfying interpersonal life, had developed an interest in the martial arts, and was significantly less anxious and withdrawn.

The only other reported case of treating a video game addict was that of Keepers (1990). A 12-year-old boy was brought by his mother for psychiatric help because her son was playing video games for four to five hours a day at an average cost of $30–50 a day over a six month period. The amount was far beyond the boy's means and he had been stealing and truanting from school in order to play. Keepers reported that the boy was physically abused by his father (as was the mother) and was placed in a residential treatment centre and given family therapy. During therapy the boy remained reluctant to discuss his home situation or his parents. In an effort to uncover some of his feelings, the boy was asked to design his own video game. Using video games as a vehicle for communication, the boy was gradually able to talk about the fear of his father and his feelings of helplessness. Family therapy was again undertaken with the eventual outcome of parental separation and return of the boy to his mother. At six month follow up, no recurrence of the boy's difficulty was noted. Keepers also considered his patient's behaviour to be reminiscent of pathological gambling.

In advice for parents, Griffiths (quoted in Neustatter, 1991) gave a common sense approach to self control based on treatment of other habits:

> do not start with 'cold turkey', but try negotiating how much your child can spend on the computer – and make sure the deal is kept. Foster friendships and try and organise other enjoyable activities to carry out with your child. Rewards for not playing can also work. And when you have done these, relax and remember that most children move quite naturally on from what may look like an addiction set for life. (p64)

For those who wish to simply curtail children's playing behaviour rather than stopping it altogether, there is now an electronic device called a 'TV Space Allowance' which can block out the television at certain times (like homework periods or late at night) (Homer, 1993). The television is activated by a secret code and once pre-set allotted time has run out, the television set automatically switches off. However, it may be relatively expensive for many families (at around £85) and it cannot be used for hand-held computer game consoles (such as Nintendo's Game Boy).

As can be seen, treatment issues for computer game addiction are still in their infancy. However, many authors (such as Keepers, 1990; Griffiths, 1991a) have noticed the similarity in psychological and behavioural consequences between excessive video game playing and pathological gambling. If video game playing is similar, then treatment of those who are dependent upon it may be helped by therapists who adapt treatment approaches from the already established treatment literature on pathological gambling.

Concluding remarks

This review has demonstrated that research into home computer games is a little studied phenomenon leaving theoretical analysis somewhat weak. It should also be reiterated that a lot of the reported findings here have been extrapolated from research into arcade video game playing. Obviously more research is needed before the debate on whether computer game playing is a generally healthy or unhealthy activity is decided. Even from sparse research, it is evident that computer games have both positive and negative aspects. If care is taken in game design, and if games are put into the right context, they have the potential to be used as training aids in classrooms and therapeutic settings, and to provide skills in psychomotor coordination in simulations of real life events, such as training recruits for the armed forces.

There is also a need for a general taxonomy of computer games, as it could be the case that particular types of games have very positive effects while other types are not so positive. For instance, the December 1992 issue of the Nintendo magazine *Total!* (Volume 1, Number 12) contained an article on 'What makes a good cart great?' ('cart'=game cartridge). The magazine identified nine different types of game in which only the final three types are essentially violent – the last three types in the following list (with examples in brackets):

- Sport simulations: this type is self explanatory. These games simulate sports such as golf, ice hockey or athletics (Hole in One, Super Tennis).
- Racers: this type could be considered a type of 'Sport Simulation' in that it simulates motor sports like Formula 1 racing (F1 Race, Top Gear).
- Adventures: this type uses fantasy settings in which the player can escape to other worlds and take on new identities (Addams Family, Zelda 3).
- Puzzlers: this type is self explanatory. These games are 'brainteasers' which often require active thinking (Tetris, Daedalian Opus).
- Weird games: these games are not 'weird' as such except they do not fit into any other category. They would be better termed 'miscellaneous' (Sim City, Pilotwings).
- Platformers: these games involve running and jumping along and onto platforms (Super Mario Brothers, Super Mario Land).
- Platform blasters: these games are 'platformers' but also involve blasting everything that comes into sight (Robocop, Batman).
- Beat 'em ups: these games involve physical violence such as punching, kicking (Street Fighter, Rival Turf).
- Shoot 'em ups: these games involve shooting and killing using various weapons (Interstellar Assault, UN Squadron).

If children and adolescents work with this degree of definitional refinement, researchers should as well. In addition to differentiating between type of game, magazine reviews also rate the games on a number of different dimensions including 'presentation', 'graphics', 'sound', 'playability', 'lastability' (short term and long term) as well as giving an overall rating. If the game players evaluate games on several dimensions then it is important for psychologists to attend to the cognitive complexity of their judgements and preferences and reflect this in the sophistication of their measures.

There are some games appearing on the market in which the player is required to manage a city, state, or world (such as Civilization, Sim City, Populous). These may provide insights into unexplored aspects of children's cognitive development. For instance, in Sim City, the player has to develop and manage a city, dealing with problems such as crime, pollution and natural disasters. Such games teach the players (albeit in a simplified way) about the choices any society has to make. It is perhaps unsurprising that Sim City has found its way into many schools in the United States as an educational tool (Homer, 1992). These games are clearly engaging players in systems management and at present there is little in the cognitive developmental literature on the child's acquisition of systems concepts. The use of these games in a research context may provide valuable insights into this little researched aspect of children's reasoning and problem solving.

However, it does appear that excessive computer game playing can have potentially damaging effects upon a minority of individuals who display compulsive and addictive behaviour, and who will do anything possible to 'feed their addiction'. Such individuals need monitoring. Using 'keyboard junkies' in research would help identify the roots and causes of addictive playing and the impact of such behaviour on family and school life. It would be clinically useful to illustrate problem cases, even following them longitudinally and recording developmental features of the adolescent computer game addict. This would help determine the variables which are salient in the acquisition, development and maintenance of computer game addiction. It may be that computer game addiction is age-related like other more obviously 'deviant' adolescent behaviours such as glue sniffing, since there is little evidence to date of computer game addiction in adults.

More research is needed into the effects of the violent content of computer games on children's subsequent behaviour. Although research has been sparse, results do seem to suggest that the playing or observing of violent games does affect young children negatively as they show increased levels of aggressive behaviour – at least in the short term (see Griffiths, 1991a). Research into the long term constant exposure to violent computer games is noticeably lacking. In the meantime, manufacturers of such games could be persuaded to make their games less aggressive by highlighting research that has shown that less aggressive games can be popular without losing their commercial appeal.

There is no doubt that for a minority of children and adolescents computer games can take up considerable time and that to all intents and purposes they are 'addicted' to them. In a study by Griffiths and Hunt (1993; 1995), seven per cent of schoolchildren claimed to spend at least 30 hours a week playing computer games. Whether the games are inherently 'good' or 'bad' is not the most pertinent question here. The issue is the effect on educational and social development of any activity (not just computer game playing) that takes up 30 hours of leisure time a week. At present we do not know the answer to such a question, but I contend that any child who engaged in any activity excessively (whether 'good' or 'bad') every day over a number of years from a young age would have their development negatively affected in some way.

Another factor to take into account is that there are nine types of computer game, many of which would appear to have little or no direct benefits to the individual playing them. Only two of the categories (puzzlers and weird games) contain games with educational components. It is perhaps some of these games that could be used in schools to foster learning and overcome some of the negative stereotypes that many people have about computer games.

The question of whether computer games are inherently 'good' or 'bad' cannot be answered at present because the available literature is sparse and conflicting. Computer game playing is thus an area for serious academic study. Psychological research could be accused of spending too much time on abstract ideas and concepts and too little time on society's developing problems. Real life problems need applied solutions and alternatives, and until there is an established body of literature on the psychological, sociological and physiological effects of computer game playing and computer game addiction, directions for education, prevention, intervention and treatment will remain limited in scope.

Is electronic entertainment hindering children's play and social development?

Elizabeth Stutz

Play

Play is natural to children; it is the means by which they get to know the world and life around them. It is far more than this, however, as we can detect when watching children at play; there is a numinous force at work which is the creative, imaginative, inventive spirit that links children to the source of life and which forms a bond between them. In the words of Gordon Sturrock from his article, 'A metaphysical journey into the meaning of play':

> What we see in children at play is a process which is spiritual, mystical in motivation, studded with mythological symbolism and linked to awareness and consciousness. (Sturrock, 1993)

From a practical viewpoint, I would like to show how I believe children are helped in their social development, and in picking up many life skills, through the socialising element and imagination which is contained in play; and how this is endangered by some of the destructive concepts and the 'hype' with which children and young people are bombarded by electronic entertainment today. And I will point the way to some possible new approaches which I believe might rectify the present bad state.

The word 'play' covers a wide variety of activities, including educational play in home and school, as well as sporting activities and structured play in institutions and youth clubs. These are all valid and have a place in children's lives. Moreover, they fulfil different needs.

There are two other kinds of play, however, which we will be thinking about here. I will call them *universal* or *cultural* play, and *spontaneous* or *creative* play. These used to be common in streets and open spaces, in the garden, the farmyard, by the village pond and in the school playground; wherever children had the space to pursue the kind of life that was their own.

The concern of many people dealing with children now – parents, educators, play workers and doctors – is that they find this kind of play has disappeared. At the age when children are normally lively and enquiring, full of enterprise and adventure, they are bored and unable to find fulfilling kinds of occupation. The question we ask is how this has come about, and whether this trend could be reversed.

About fifteen years ago Iona Opie undertook a study, which she reported in diary form in her book *The People in the Playground* (1994). The games she describes are similar to the ones Breughel painted in his famous picture of 'Children at Play' three hundred years ago: the sort of games most of us will remember with delight from our own childhood.

UNICEF documented these and many others in *Games of the World* (Grunfeld, 1982) in which their origins are shown. They are centuries old, springing from the daily lives of people in many different parts of the world and in different cultures. They are the common heritage of children the world over: games such as leapfrog, piggy-back, skipping, hopscotch, jacks, marbles, hoops, stilts, grandmother's footsteps, dipping and others.

Yet in the short years since Opie carried out her study, these games have disappeared, or almost disappeared, from school playgrounds, streets and open spaces. There have been complaints from schools in all parts of this country to the effect that children are bored and no longer know how to occupy themselves and that the play of boys is becoming increasingly violent.

Apart from the fun and good exercise these games provide, can they be said to be of value in children's social development? I will give a few examples to show that this is the case.

In leapfrog, the player who leaps is totally dependent on the one who supports her or him and there is therefore a strong element of trust on the part of the one player, and responsibility, supportiveness and dependability by the other. There is body contact which makes for trust and good relationships; skill is needed by both players; no one wins; they succeed or fail together; there is an element of adventure, because a fair amount of courage is needed; the players' aim is to succeed together and they both enjoy this; and girls and boys are involved together, on an equal footing, patiently taking turns.

Piggy-back has similar characteristics, with trust and dependability being uppermost. Joint endeavour is part of the fun. If the children do not succeed they both fall over and the fun continues with rolling on the ground together!

Skipping can be done alone or in twos or more. When two share a rope and skip together, success depends on their turning the rope in unison; different skills are needed. There are various singing rhymes to help them keep in time, and for counting. When two hold the rope for others to jump or run through, the two holding the rope need to work with each other; they need to watch the skipper and keep in time with him or her. The more children take part, the more they each depend on the skills of the others and the greater the coordination needed; success depends on each individually, as well as on the group acting well together; success again is shared.

Because the children in all these and similar games are working together and interacting with each other, the players learn to find solutions to their problems together, and to work out their differences. They communicate on different levels and find out how other people think and act, as well as getting to know themselves. They very rarely quarrel on these occasions.

There is a link between these games and folk-tales which lies in the ancient singing games, nursery rhymes and riddles; also in seasonal practices such as dancing round the maypole, the witches and magic at Hallowe'en and Santa Claus and the reindeer. Although these vary in different cultures, many of them have equivalents in other countries and religions.

Bruno Bettelheim, in his work *The Uses of Enchantment* (1975), considers these practices to be of the utmost importance to children; he describes them as being '...very much the result of common consciousness and unconscious content.' The games contain something of a dream quality and symbolism which Bettelheim also sees in fairy tales and which Jung refers to when explaining his theory of archetypes.

There is a similar suggestion in the book *British Folk Tales and Legends: A Sampler* (Briggs, 1977) in which the folklorist, Katherine Briggs, links magic, myths, beast-fables, giants, folk-tales, folk-songs, rhymes, traditional games, folk-drama, nursery rhymes and riddles.

The kind of activity that I have called creative or spontaneous play contains a similar element, but in this children invent their own games and occupations. It is what they usually describe as 'mucking around'. Paul Bonel describes and illustrates this in his book *Playing for Real* (1993). Play for Life, the organisation I helped to found, decided to call this *real play*, and is seeking to revitalise this kind of play in its leaflet campaign and travelling exhibition called *Rescuing Real Play*. It is what children do when free-wheeling and when they have some space, either indoors or out. They create their own devices and initiatives and often find their own materials. The fewer sophisticated props they have, the more inventive they become. They find time to wonder and to reflect; they gain confidence and self-reliance, they get to know themselves and their playmates through interaction. They act out everyday scenes and personal experiences. In this way they work through their emotional needs and the traumas that are part of daily life.

Children need to be in touch with nature and its processes: to see injured birds fallen from trees; their pet produce a family; acorns rotting in the ground and sending up new shoots; life and death linked with joy and grieving and loving. With these kinds of experience, a nucleus of wisdom is formed, growing into a storehouse of resources to draw on as they get older.

Figures 1 and 2 illustrate how I visualise that children perceive the world they live in and how this shapes their development. In Figure 1 the children's feet are firmly planted on the earth. They see the cycle of life; the birth and death of plants and animals. They feel secure; their mind and spirit are free to rise above it and to enjoy imaginative play. In Figure 2 the blocks represent the child's choices. They are encircled by unfriendly forces. The child's mind and spirit are trapped. Stagnation and boredom set in.

Liberating and wonderful as technology can be, it must remain an instrument, and never become a substitute for real play or real life. The child should experience actual reality, not virtual reality.

Saturation entertainment

Saturation entertainment has taken over children's playtime and home life, so that they suffer the consequences of being overwhelmed and brutalised by entertainment, and are exposed to concepts totally unsuitable for and inimical to their stage of development. These present a distorted view of the world; children are robbed of the carefree hours in which they could be enjoying the nourishing and creative forces of play. Why is this so? Children's leisure time has been made the subject of intense commercial competition. The richest and most powerful industries and interest groups, such as the ever-expanding communications industry, the electronic entertainments and music

Figure 1:   The world of universal play and imaginative play

industries, Hollywood and Silicon Valley, the toy, computer and consumer goods and food empires, have together in a loose conglomerate taken over as their domain the market of childhood and youth; they decide what children will play, read, eat, wear, admire, hate, how they behave to each other, to their parents and authority and who their role models are to be; this contrivance is then sold as the youth culture.

The effect this has on children is illustrated in Sherry Turkle's words:

Figure 2: The world of the electronic child

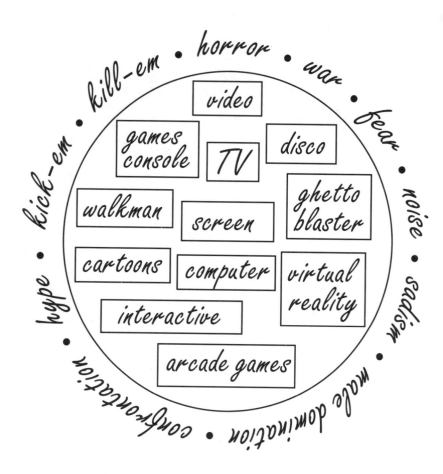

When you play a video game you enter into the world of the programmers who made it. You have to do more than identify with the character on the screen. You must act for it. Identification through action has a special kind of hold. Like playing a sport, it puts people into a highly focused, and highly charged state of mind. For many people, what is being pursued in the video game is not just a score, but an altered state. (Turkle, 1984)

I found this observation confirmed in my encounters with a large proportion of the 500 children I interviewed who followed games about combat closely (Stutz, 1991). When interviewing children on their preferred computer games I found the ones containing fighting to be unanimously the favourites; and when asked what they understood of the storyline in a game, all they could say was, 'you gotto kick 'em and punch 'em; you gotto kill 'em'.

This is in fact what the most popular games amount to. Not only are the players instructed to kill, but they are shown a wide range of weapons with which to carry this out, told how to use everyday objects, as well as learning all the relevant punches, kicks, chops, hair pulling and similar strategies. Children take this all intensely seriously. The aim is to carry out the killing with as few strokes as possible, in sharp competition with their peers. There are numerous magazines and telephone helplines which give advice on how to proceed. The player must follow a prescribed course and cannot use his own ideas; the only skill needed is speed of movement in the fingers and hand–eye coordination. Another worrying factor was their total involvement with the killer and the extent to which they identified with him. They appeared to lose all sense of reality.

Eugene Provenzo, Professor of Education at Miami University, in his book *Video Kids: Making Sense of Nintendo* refers to Turkle's book. He says:

> Additional questions are raised by Turkle concerning what happens to the individual as he enters into the simulation and assumes the role of the movie character or sports figure. In this process, there is more than simply an identification with the character on the screen. (Provenzo, 1991)

Video films

I found that the effect on children of what they saw on the screen was enormous. I was struck by the seriousness with which they took their entertainment, the intensity, viciousness and explicitness, which was worse than I had anticipated. In order to acquaint myself with the children's experience I watched some of the video films, thus to be able to enter to a small extent into the world by which they were captivated – the continual flow of scenes of brutality and sadism, accompanied by loud screaming and gruesome side effects, are watched for hours on end, daily.

The most striking feature about their comments was the terrible fear that most of them had suffered when quite young, when they had forced themselves to watch programmes on television or video, which they found truly terrifying, and how they had hardened themselves, so that by the age of seven or eight they might be able to watch a whole programme without suffering pangs of fear or nightmares and then no longer needed to be ashamed or ridiculed.

What are the concepts that are being taught by means of computer games, the majority of cartoons and video nasties and the TV films based on 'heroes'? That the first chief means of getting what you want is through violence; any available object can and should be used as a weapon; life of others is valueless; pain is non-existent; mental cruelty is 'OK'; physical power in the male is to be admired above all else; women are there for the pleasure and convenience of men.

This list sounds so crude that it appears oversimplistic and exaggerated. However, when studying the material that is presented to children, these are the characteristics that emerge. I was not able to detect any elements that detracted from the starkness of these messages.

Professor Marsha Kinder, member of several video game review panels, believes that games:

> are different from other media because they actively engage children in violent acts. It is worse than TV or movies. It communicates the message that the only way to be empowered is through violence. (Kinder, 1993)

Of the many complex and tangled issues involved in the question of the electronic child and the child's social development I would like to consider one in some more depth as this itself touches many facets of life. It is children's perception of their sexuality and of the role of both sexes in the home, at school, in the world of work and the workplace and society generally, as well as their relationship to each other. What role models are they given, what guidance as to appropriate ways of conducting these relationships?

As we have seen, girls and boys often play together in cultural games. They gradually and naturally become aware of their sexuality and notice the differences between each other. As Opie discovered, they speak quite openly and innocently of these things and delight in naming parts of the body and bodily functions which makes them feel knowledgeable and important (Opie, 1994). This is a healthy and natural way for them to grow up in their pre-pubescent years and if their development were allowed to continue in this way their relations with the opposite sex as they grow older is likely to be civilised. However, as much of their spare time is now filled with mass entertainment, they are powerfully influenced by the way women and men are portrayed in computer games, video films and television. From this they will gain their self-image, as well as the attitude to the opposite sex.

According to Provenzo's study of attitudes shown toward women in their entertainment, one third of the most popular computer games, which included 'such sports as car racing, basketball, football and professional boxing', showed girls as being helpless victims, having been kidnapped and having to be rescued by the heroic male, and playing only a subsidiary role, having neither name nor personality. As he puts it:

> Women...are often cast as individuals who are acted upon rather than as initiators of action...women are depicted as victims in the games. Thus games not only socialize women to be dependent, but also condition men to assume dominant gender roles. It is not video games alone that discriminate against women; other media, including television, popular magazines, and radio, reflect similar hegemomic forces at work in culture. What is important in the case of video games is how blatant these types of discriminatory attitudes are in terms of the content of the games. (Provenzo, 1991)

Provenzo concludes the chapter, given over entirely to this theme, by claiming that women suffer a double injustice because they are being both sex-typed and are also disadvantaged in terms of their future education and job potential.

When interviewing children on their thoughts about computer games, I found this confirmed. The girls in general were less keen than the boys on computers because they saw the computer world slanted towards the male perspective and were therefore discouraged from taking an interest in them. The girls who did persevere did so in order to keep up with the boys, because they may well have sensed that they were at a disadvantage.

The idea of casting boys in the role of the hero is, however, not to the advantage of boys either. It is out of keeping with the present world when girls' talents are increasingly being recognised and they are in many cases outstripping boys in school performance, while their fathers are more often being seen in a caring and gentle role, and the mother may be the dominant figure. Nor do boys of a more gentle disposition fit comfortably into the tough hero role. They are the ones most likely to be the target of the bully boy who is acting out the role model he sees on the screen.

From time to time there are startling reports of the large number of teenage pregnancies and of rape by teenage boys, yet little time is given to looking for the causes for these conditions, or the consequences. The editors of *Video Violence and Children* state:

It is a matter of great concern that in the formative years, from the ages of seven to 17, 45 per cent of children should have seen video films which would legally be classed as obscene in [Britain] on account of the morbid, sadistic and repugnant nature of the violence they portray. The first knowledge of sexual life acquired by these children may come from viewing films in which sexual conduct is inextricably entwined with violence, hatred, coercion and the humiliation of women in particular. (Barlow and Hill, 1985)

And in Michael Medved's book, *Hollywood vs. America: Popular Culture and the War on Traditional Values*, the author, who is an American film critic, writer and broadcaster, takes serious issue with Hollywood and its portrayal of sex and attitude to the family. He devotes a whole chapter to how, as he puts it, Hollywood is promoting promiscuity. He quotes a large number of extremely obscene passages from popular songs which, he claims, must be heard many times over by millions of young people (Medved, 1992).

No thought is given to the effects these programmes must inevitably have on young adolescents who receive the message that sexual activity is expected of them at an early age, nor of the consequences of so-called 'unwanted pregnancies'; that these will lead to unwanted babies and then to children and young mothers who will start their lives with a great handicap and are likely to have to suffer extreme hardships for many years to come.

Some protagonists of the present fashion in electronic entertainment claim that it is the historic continuation of ancient mythology which has progressed in the last century through comics and cartoons to the present technological manifestation, and that this represents a kind of triumph or liberation of man's spirit and a channel for children's fantasy, as presented by Stephen Rennie (Rennie, 1993). While psychiatrists, such as Bettelheim, and folklorists like Briggs, see a strong connection between play and the world of mythology, they both deplore the distortions which the genuine stories undergo in the process of being exploited for commercial profit, or the fabrication of new ones. Some of these new myths may have certain artistic merit; however such large numbers of programmes and games are required that it results in the production of stories that are simply used as a backdrop for brutality and killing. As to the fantasy element, which much is made of, this is for the most part so crude, grotesque and overpowering that the child's own imaginative capacities become overwhelmed and they become habituated to the kind of images presented.

I would add a word about the danger of continuing outmoded traditions. The tradition of the mythological hero, the superman, has in the course of time developed to such an extent that the physical strength of the male and his unquestioned domination, has come to pose serious problems in the real world. Could there not be a link between Hitler's passion for the Germanic Nibelungen Saga – and Wagner's rendering of this in four epic operas – and Hitler's obsession with the idea of a master race, with its disastrous consequences in history? The early heroes fought one-to-one battles and adhered to strict rules of chivalry in a male-dominated world. Is the modern version of the hero-myth represented in modern times by the development of increasingly advanced technology in mass warfare – by the dropping of cluster bombs on unseen civilians, and laying of mines in agricultural land – are these the extension of the spirit of the ancient myths? Could the inventors of these weapons have been inspired by the enjoyment of comics and cartoons in their childhood?

These are not rhetorical questions. If the present climate in electronic entertainment continues and children continue to be taught these distorted perceptions and false values, so that a whole generation grows up separated from its cultural roots and innate creativity, will not an even more serious threat to society exist? This is particularly significant when seen in the context of what Provenzo writes about the military uses of computer games. He discusses the uses to which these are put in army training in the United States and says:

> In the military one is expected to take orders and obey them without question. The enemy is rarely seen...but by planes dropping bombs on anonymous populations....Video games provide an almost perfect simulation for the actual conditions of warfare....In contrast to the actual conditions of war, where surrender, compromise or truce may be the best choice, video games promote total war and aggression....The individuals being taught are part of an anonymous machine. (Provenzo, 1991)

What hope for the future?

I believe the situation might be reversed if the relevant parts of the entertainments industry, the planners and designers, changed from offering passivity on the part of the player, and death as the motivating force of the game, to a mould-breaking and fresh kind of game in which the players were set a variety of creative and life-affirming tasks, preferably away from the screen. Alternatively the equipment could be used in novel, challenging and constructive ways so that, rather than exploiting the weak, cruel and destructive side of the child's nature, the positive human and loving attributes were engaged.

It must finally be said that the electronic entertainments industry is not solely responsible for the disappearance of play. Above all, society as a whole needs to recognise its responsibility to provide a pleasing and inviting environment near children's homes, where they can play and lead adventurous lives and pursue all the kinds of activities needed for their wholesome cultural and social development. Until this happens, children will continue to regard killing games as their chief adventure and look for their amusement while sitting around an electronic instrument.

Part 3: Computers in education

Introduction

Tim Gill

How are teachers and pupils using computers, and how are computers changing education? Some argue that computers might make some tasks too easy for children, as (it is claimed) happened when calculators were first allowed into the classroom. Graveney School's pupils are alive to these fears; Debbie Lovell worries that using computers for art classes might mean that 'you wouldn't learn to shade or how to paint properly.' Her fellow pupil Shem Pennant feels that 'people can get too reliant on IT, and become unable to do independent research.' Against this danger, computers (like calculators) can take out much of the unnecessary drudgery of school work. Victor John from Graveney School writes that 'being dyslexic I find it very easy when I have completed my work on my computer just to put on the spell checker.' He believes computers 'have contributed to my improved spelling and that I have become more confident in lessons when a teacher asks me to spell words in front of the class.' Indeed Department for Education and Employment (DFEE) figures suggest that computers are making their biggest impact on the education of pupils with special educational needs; in 1993–4 both the number of computers per pupil and the expenditure on IT equipment was twice as high in special schools as in secondary schools (DFEE, 1995).

But statistics and the views of individual pupils only tell part of the story. If we want to look for profound changes in educational practice, we need to think about the conceptual frameworks or models within which teachers and pupils are using computers. Charles Crook's paper offers such a set of frameworks, which have their roots in psychological theories of learning (Scrimshaw, 1993). Crook assesses four: the computer-as-tutor, computer-as-pupil, computer-as-resource and computer-as-fabric. Of these four frameworks, Crook argues that the first three are unlikely to transform 'the community structure of typical school life', because computers cannot provide the kind of contextual support that is needed in learning. It is interesting to note that these three frameworks cover most of the computer applications currently taking place in schools, as exemplified in the good practice described in the contributions from Colin Wells and Helen Rickards. These frameworks would also embrace almost all educational use of computers at home, where arguably the lack of parental familiarity can inhibit effective use (a factor which schools could help alleviate by providing guidance and hands-on experience for technophobic parents).

But Crook makes a different assessment of the computer-as-fabric model. Computers may yet revolutionise education, he feels, by becoming the medium in which learning takes place. In this scenario, 'virtual schools' would allow classroom-type exchanges to take place in the comfort of one's own terminal, supported by on-line multi-media resources. These ideas are echoed by another educational theorist, Peter Scrimshaw, who sees computers as offering 'a medium that creates new possibilities for learning and communication between teachers and learners' (Scrimshaw, 1993). However, Crook claims that public libraries already offer much of what is claimed for virtual schools, yet hardly seem to excite the same enthusiasm amongst educationalists. Curiously enough, Shem Pennant from Graveney School addresses just this comparison. But for him, computers are 'much, much more interesting!' He adds that 'they are also much more accessible than a local library, as they do not have odd opening hours and overdue charges.' Of course, this accessibility is only available at a cost that is beyond the reach of many families; as Shem's fellow pupil Joel Prager asks, 'why does the computer industry continue to produce equipment which is too expensive for us to afford?'

Shem's glowing endorsement of multi-media technology hints at another question about computers in education; how much of children's undoubted enthusiasm is just the 'gee whizz' effect, set to vanish as soon as computers take their humdrum place alongside pencils and books in children's lives? In response to this question, the children's keenness seems to stem from more than the sheer novelty value of having a new toy in the classroom. Both Wells and Rickards emphasise how computers foster collaboration between pupils, thereby keeping them motivated. Indeed Scrimshaw argues that computers produce clear learning results through the use of 'the socially oriented process values of group work and collaboration' (Scrimshaw, 1993). Alex Wood-craft from Graveney School relates how 'in other subjects we have to be quiet and sit at our desks – it can get very boring. But in IT we work as members of a team, swapping ideas, discussing projects – reaching the best solutions together.' In this way, computers offer a way out of the 'teacher's dilemma' described by some educationalists: namely 'how teachers both achieve externally set goals and do so by learner-centred methods' (Scrimshaw, 1993).

Schools of the future

Charles Crook

Will computers transform the experience of going to school? Should we anticipate a new generation of electronic pupils? Clearly, many commentators do believe that dramatic changes are imminent. Here is what Professor Seymour Papert proposes when invited to predict how schools will change under the influence of technology:

> There won't be schools in the future...I think the computer will blow up the school. That is, the school defined as something where there are classes, teachers running exams, people structured in groups by age, follow a curriculum – all of that. The whole system is based on a set of structural concepts that are incompatible with the presence of the computer. (Papert, 1984)

Papert is well placed to judge these matters. This distinguished MIT scientist enjoys great respect among teachers – both for his vision of education as described in the book *Mindstorms* and for his development of Logo, an ingenious way for young children to program computers in the classroom. Papert's predictions deserve careful attention. Will schools as we know them disappear?

Future-guessing is not a much respected occupation, but there can still be real value in it. That value lies in helping us deal better with events in the present. In an arena such as education, subtle political and economic forces inevitably will be guiding the course of any reform. Speculating about the future causes us to bring those influences into sharper focus: we are thereby made more sensitive to their workings. A practical consequence follows: our speculations may prove useful in suggesting priorities for whoever must sponsor critical research on educational matters. Indeed, in the present essay I will converge on some examples of current research that I believe illustrate what those priorities might be.

Lessons from media research

So, future-guessing should really be about orienting us towards the present. Yet the way we go about that guesswork may involve a certain degree of looking behind us; a certain consideration of the past. For in wondering how new technology will change education, we might learn from looking at the broader history of how mass media have entered our lives. The American academic Brian Winston has written about this topic in relation to contemporary communications and broadcasting technologies. In his book *Misunderstanding Media* (Winston, 1986), he traces their technical development and the patterns of their adoption into modern societies. Two striking messages emerge from his research. The first is that, typically, new media are directed towards mass usage only very slowly – despite the energetic claims and predictions often surrounding them. For example, a prototype television existed in 1936 but it was not until the late 1950s that television became a genuine mass media. This sluggish industrial development invariably reflects resistent manoeuvering by established commercial interests – with their investment in older and competing media.

The second message of Winston's research is contained in what he terms 'the law of suppression of radical potential'. This alerts us to the tendency for new media to reproduce existing forms of creative expression. Again, the case of television is a good example. Certainly, it has reconfigured the patterns of our social lives (family life in particular). Yet, it is hard to see the content of television as genuinely innovative. Consider its formats: we find theatrical, stage-set conventions dominating that 'novel' TV creation, the situation comedy; the classic newspaper tradition dictates a photogenic TV journalist reading copy; spectator sport gets reproduced as the outside broadcast; the fairground booth becomes the game show. As Winston notes, the creative variety evident in the different presentational modes of Eastern cultures are hardly characteristic of our own traditions of mass media. Again, this suppression of radical potential must be understood partly in terms of the exercising of entrenched commercial interests. At times of innovation, those with substantial investments in production techniques for the already established media, will want to see their interests protected and redeployed within any new media opportunity.

At the very least, this lesson of history should caution us not to talk up the likely impact of a further new media (that is, computers). In particular, the impact of computers on schools may not be quite as fast or as radical as some educational prophets will have us believe. It might also lead us to anticipate that what this technology gets used for by teachers will tend to reproduce existing habits of educational practice. Fortunately, again there is documentary research we may turn to in order to check this expectation against history. In his book *Teachers and Machines*, Larry Cuban traces how various technologies have been appropriated into classrooms across this century. It is clear from his research that most modern mass media have at some time been regarded as likely to 'revolutionise' education. For example, the great Thomas Edison commented in 1922:

> I believe that the motion picture is destined to revolutionise our educational system and that in a few years it will supplant largely, if not entirely, the use of textbooks. (Quoted in Cuban, 1986)

Here is another example of misguided prophecy. One textbook published in 1945 was devoted to teaching with radio; it was able to declare:

> The time will come when a portable radio receiver will be as common in the classroom as is the blackboard. Radio instruction will be integrated into school life as an accepted educational medium. (Quoted in Cuban, 1986)

Cuban's book opens with a compelling photograph: it shows a group of children lined up at desks, attentively facing a teacher who holds a pointer to a blackboard – but all this taking place on an aeroplane. Curiously then, there was a time when even powered flight was thought to have a revolutionary potential for certain aspects of the curriculum. Yet this photograph strongly reinforces Winston's principle outlined above. Radical potential gets suppressed: the photograph shows us existing teaching formats and conventions simply getting reproduced within new technological opportunities. Cuban begins to document this for the particular case of the computer, developing the same general point about the fate of this 'machine' for teachers. However, we could feel uneasy about this extrapolation of his basic thesis. Cuban's book was written in the early 1980s and it may be felt that information technology has advanced in such unexpected ways that any law of suppression of radical potential will be violated for the case of teachers appropriating computers. Consequently, I shall move next to reflect on the recent history of computer use in education to see if the picture does indeed define a break with the history of teachers using machines. I shall identify and evaluate three orientations to the technology that have each served as a focal point for arguments about the revolutionary potential of computers for teaching. We may consider whether they have delivered – or are delivering – the radical promise they have each suggested.

Frameworks for change: the computer as tutor

When we think casually about organised education, we will doubtless bring to mind this core image: a teacher and a pupil (expert and novice) in some sort of directed person-to-person encounter. Perhaps we will conjure up a metaphor whereby what the expert knows is channelled into the novice, thanks to a certain species of skilful communication ('instruction'). In fact, many educational theorists would be uneasy with this didactic model of teaching. Yet it probably informs the oldest and most ambitious model of applying computers to education: the 'computer as tutor'. In its simplest realisation, this model frames teaching as a three-part encounter. First, a problem or challenge is set (by the teacher), next a response is thereby elicited (from the pupil), and finally feedback (from the teacher) completes this cycle.

While this perspective on teaching may well reflect common sense understanding of the activity, it also gains academic respectability from the theorising of some psychologists. In particular, the movement of behaviourism in psychology encourages this model of teaching. In fact, it was behaviourists who designed the precursor to the modern computer-as-tutor – namely, the 'teaching machine' of the 1950s. These devices could relentlessly feed pupils initiation–response–feedback cycles of just the kind sketched above. The modern computerised version is much more sophisticated and it would now be termed an 'intelligent tutoring system' (ITS). Moreover, while it owes much to psychological theorising, the contemporary theoretical inspiration comes more from the modern movement of cognitive psychology. One of the giants of this tradition – Herb Simon – captures a certain view of the teaching process in his (admittedly off the cuff) comment:

> I find it terribly frustrating, trying to transfer my knowledge and skill to another human head. I'd like to open the lid and stuff the program in. (Simon, 1983)

This remark exercises the pervasive model of teaching as some sort of 'stuffing in' of knowledge. It also alerts us to the modern psychologists' preoccupation with computational models of mind – that is, with claims that to be knowledgeable is to be equipped with some sort of head 'program'. Yet this approach meets two problems when applied to teaching (and the machines that try to embody it). First, the implicit analysis of knowledge as discrete, stored representations is questionable. Therefore, it would certainly be controversial within psychology to claim that teaching merely must involve optimising the transfer of such material between two 'information systems' (teacher and pupil). However, I will not dwell on the particular debates that this issue has given rise to. Consider instead the second problem with intelligent tutoring systems: namely, the idea that the interpersonal communication making up a tutorial relationship is something that can be simulated in a computer-based format. Can computers support a teaching dialogue? Only up to a point: some software may have made respectable approximations to some of what goes on during tutoring – and these approximations may well be useful for certain educational purposes – but the core of any effective, sustained tutorial encounter defies this mechanical reproduction.

We get a sense of this from an interesting study by Mark Lepper (Lepper and others, 1993) in which the detailed talk and interaction of teachers was documented while they were working in class. This record was compared with the style of interaction supported by computer-based tutors. The difference between the human and the machine versions is striking. Those precise patterns of feedback, correction, diagnosis and demonstration that ITS designers strive to achieve simply does not seem to characterise what expert tutors actually do. What teachers do that may be especially helpful is interact in ways that are studiously chosen to be incomplete or otherwise imperfect; interventions chosen because they are provocative of further engagement by the learner. Such cultivated imprecision is a powerful and stimulating form of instructional exchange, but it is hard to mobilise and control. It depends upon that distinctively human capacity that psychologists term 'intersubjectivity': the capacity to project psychological states (such as intentions, beliefs and desires) into other people's minds. Effective teaching may be so tiring simply because it calls upon a sustained investment in 'mindreading' pupils in just this sense. Doing so is what will allow instructional intervention to be well tuned to the learner's knowledge, interests and needs at any particular moment; doing so exercises a uniquely human capability.

In sum, the computer-as-tutor model has some merit. It can be made to work, and it has been – at least, for teaching certain skills under certain circumstances. Without doubt, it retains a natural appeal among practitioners and policy makers: it is estimated that over half of the money spent on educational software in American schools is spent on 'Integrated Learning Systems', the current classroom realisation of this model. However, the impossibility of simulating true intersubjectivity within a computer program does render the computer-as-tutor model limited in its revolutionary promise. Thus, we must remain vigilant in respect of predictions of the following sort:

> In a few more years, millions of school children will have access to what Philip of Macedon's son Alexander enjoyed as a royal prerogative: the personal services of a tutor as well-informed and responsive as Aristotle. (Suppes, 1966)

This judgement on the future of computer-based instruction came from a most distinguished innovator in the teaching machine tradition (Patrick Suppes); yet it is sobering to note that his prediction was made exactly 30 years ago.

Frameworks for change: the computer as pupil

Seymour Papert was mentioned earlier. His great contribution to thinking about educational technology has been to foreground the idea that computers might play the role of 'pupil' – rather than teacher – in the instructional relationship. The idea is to regard the computer as a tool which the learner may come to control – or 'teach' to do things. Because it is such a general-purpose machine, the computer can offer a variety of different environments for the learner to fashion in creative ways. Briefly, Papert's argument is as follows. If you want to learn, say, French, you go to a place where knowing the language allows you to get things done (for instance, France!). All areas of the curriculum should enjoy similar opportunities. So, if we are concerned with teaching, say, mathematics, then what is needed is some kind of 'mathsland': some maths equivalent to the place where French goes on. Computers can furnish such 'microworlds'. In using them, learners can be empowered to make the machine do something purposeful and interesting – achievements that educators will arrange to depend on their pupils exercising some principled domain of knowledge, such as mathematics. Thus, Papert's Turtle Logo invites children to control the movements of a robot (floor 'turtle') through experimenting with ideas in arithmetic, geometry and algebra as these ideas are required by a simple control language supported on the computer. When equipped with Logo, the computer becomes a 'pupil' that the schoolchild teaches to do things – in this case, through the application of mathematical ideas.

Such microworlds can be very open-ended in terms of the creative scope they allow. Alternatively the learner may be confronted with a more closed environment (a 'simulation') but, still, the aim is to use principled knowledge to control and thereby understand some underlying system. Much research now indicates that computers used in this way can provide very powerful and engaging experiences. However, research is also clear in showing that serious learning from them does not occur spontaneously. It is not enough simply to be exposed to these tools. In short, there is no 'magic bullet' treatment on offer here: microworlds and simulations do not cultivate knowledge in the learner without an important degree of contextual support.

There are at least two kinds of support that are going to be significant – and difficult to build into technology. First, any possible exploration of the microworld has to be motivated. Learners have to derive an urge and some initial direction for the computer-based explorations that are in principle available to them. Second, their microworld activities have to be interpreted. Learners need their achievements to be located in broader frameworks of knowledge. These are aspects of the learning environment that, again, I believe depend upon the intersubjective capabilities of real teachers. They depend on sympathetic interventions from more expert people in the learning environment. Such people will build upon their own understanding of the learner's experiences so far in some knowledge domain: this will entail reacting to perhaps very recent, particular experiences but also it will entail making connections with a longer history of what the learner already knows and cares about.

The framework of computer-as-pupil can certainly have a real impact on educational practice. However, the reach of its impact will depend upon practitioners fully embracing an educational idea: namely, that knowledge must arise out of purposeful and creative exploration by the learner. This is not a new idea. Computers did not cause it to be discovered, but the technology does encourage it – by providing powerful new vehicles to support such creative explorations. So, computers might well mediate a significant shift of educational attitudes in this direction. Any such changes might then be regarded as 'revolutionary'. However, this is not revolution in any strong sense of Papert's 'blowing up the school'. As in my remarks about computer-as-tutor, I have concluded again that the interpersonal dimension of the teacher–learner relationship will not be readily displaced. In the present case of computer-as-pupil, one would want to add that this precious social dimension within teaching is complex. It does not only involve the one-to-one exchanges of traditional tuition. The social dimension also involves a broader community context. That is, the need to motivate and interpret learning experiences is most effectively derived and delivered from within dynamic social organisations: the communities that are created by classrooms.

Frameworks for change: the computer as resource

My third anchor point for viewing the possibility of revolutionary changes to schooling is captured in the phrase 'resource-based learning'. Writing about this, Josie Taylor and Diane Laurillard (1995) define the idea as 'open access, self-directed learning from a large information source'. This framework entails orienting the learner towards knowledge resources and inviting the various skills of posing questions, searching, and systematising. Thus, in the sense discussed above (in relation to computer-as-pupil), the learner is viewed as active. What the learner comes to know is discovered and negotiated – it is not merely received. Computers have become a significant feature in resource-based practice. This is particularly so since the appearance of multi-media presentation formats and the development of non-linear procedures (hypermedia) for reading such information databases. What this means in practice is well enough captured in remarks by the computer industry giant Bill Gates in a column carried by *The Guardian* newspaper. In the following passage he is speculating about a child learning from various compact disc titles playable on her computer:

> A girl wondering about the solar system could use a title that let her choose any planet or moon she wanted to study. She could see photos, listen to narrations, examine diagrams and read details. If she didn't know something such as the difference between a planet and a moon, she could look it up. In order for this to work, abundant information must be available almost instantly.

Much of the current enthusiasm for educational technology is focussed on the capability of computers for collecting and organising such 'abundant information'. It is right that we should recognise here a revolutionary potential: in the sense that appropriating multi-media resource bases should shift the culture of formal education towards stressing greater autonomy for learners. However, again this does not imply some prospect of liberating pupils from the institutional structures of school. As identified above, there are conditions for learning that are not readily embodied in the technology itself. Exploratory experiences do need to be motivated and interpreted. Why should Gates' child 'wonder about the solar system' in the first place? Moreover, anything she discovers from exploring computer-based information resources does not become her 'knowledge' until such fragments of information are integrated into the existing body of personal understandings that defines 'what she knows'. Such integration depends upon teachers having access to pupils' histories of learning, and being inclined to support pupils in making the necessary integrating moves.

There is a further demand associated with such resource-based learning. Searching and systematising information databases calls upon skills that are not just intuitively available. The abilities of framing appropriate questions and then exercising effective investigative strategies are abilities that themselves will have to be nurtured and supported. That support will need to be organised by others who are more experienced and who, again, have understanding of what learners already know.

These observations converge upon the same conclusions we have reached in considering other fashionable frameworks for conceptualising computers in education. The computer-as-resource does invite reconfiguration of the activities and relationships that go to make up formal education. However, the community structure of typical school life is not inherently under threat from this technology. Yet, I believe there is need to consider one more framework. In this final case, we may feel less confident of reaching the same conclusion.

Frameworks for change: the computer as fabric

The idea hinted at in the above heading concerns how technology can function as a central medium for sustaining the communication that must go on during learning: that is, it can transform the very fabric of educational environments. Such a prospect arises from the manner in which computers now integrate a number of technologies that, previously, were regarded as separate. This integration is so far-reaching that it no longer seems right to talk of 'the' computer in education – the image of a circumscribed, self-contained machine no longer seems to fit.

I have already mentioned multi-media information databases; they represent one form of media integration (text, sound, pictures and animation). However, the power of such resources is extended still further by their integration with computer networks: individual machines linked together in order to allow effortless transfer of material between them. These communications can span international distances. They are radically changing the way users of computers work and interact. Indeed, one key industry player promotes its products through the slogan 'the computer IS the network'.

This knitting together of multi-media resources and communications technology is reaching schools. Many pupils now have access to Internet – the backbone of the current global computer network. Contemporary practices on the Internet suggest some ways in which educational resourcing may develop. At the very least, what has been achieved so far on this network suggests a limited future for compact disc technology and other discrete storage devices. Information previously traded on physical media can now be delivered directly (to home or school) through the cabling of some networking infrastructure (although the lessons of Winston's research on other mass media – mentioned earlier – does hint that there will be substantial industrial resistence to this radical change in delivery technologies). Gates' young girl exploring the solar system might now do so from the convenience of some simple receiving device attached to a suitably fast communications network. That receiving device might be in her own home. Again, it looks as if such a learner might in the future be liberated from the constraints of institutionalised schooling. For in the case of the networked environment, the technology is furnishing the traditional educational resources, but also is acting as the site for whatever interpersonal communications might be needed to complement these resources.

I have been arguing here that it is the community structure of school that defines its precious feature; a feature that we cannot expect to embody in computer programs. However, if educational technologists wish to preserve the interpersonal aspect of schooling, their options are not restricted to a simulation approach. Making computers act as if they actually were people may not be the most productive strategy. Computer networking suggests a different technological transformation of the school and one that attempts to respect the social dimension of education. It could be one as profound as any (rashly) promised from developments within the traditional frameworks we have been considering. What I have termed computer-as-fabric might be regarded as a development likely to fracture the familiar social and material nature of the school. For it requires us to contemplate the notion of a 'virtual school' – an institution that does not depend on the traditional congregation of its participants. In the virtual school, computer networks certainly distribute familiar resources ('texts' for learners); but they also promise a communication infrastructure, in which some sort of community of shared purpose and interpretative effort might be sustained. That, at least, is the possibility.

Confronting this prospect, we might reflect on a certain kind of observation that could arise in any enthusiastic discussion of what networking is all about. Imagine a resource that offers to a child the following: a place close at hand where they may go at will, finding there the full breadth of human knowledge concentrated and made available in text, pictures and other accessible formats. Moreover, the resources on offer are kept regularly up to date, reflecting events in the world at large as they change on a daily basis. Finally, this place provides expert human assistance: individuals interested in helping you find what you need to know. It is somewhere you may even meet up with others who share your own interests.

Of course such places are real enough already: they are called 'public libraries'. It is interesting that they embody many of the characteristics used to promote the power of the Internet for educators. If the appeal to children of public libraries is anything to go by, then we can expect the development of virtual schools to be hard work. Moreover as management of Internet moves from government to commercial agents, so we can expect accessing this resource also to become expensive work.

Naturally, enthusiasts will argue that the Internet is not really like the tradition of public libraries. It will be claimed that it represents a real qualitative advance on the institutional structures we already know: it is more interactive, more user-friendly, more vivid and so on. I am not yet convinced by such arguments. In particular, I am not persuaded by the American pioneer metaphors that are invoked to describe the experience of using the Internet – surfing, cruising, electronic frontiers and so on. For, as the American journalist Geoffrey Nunberg notes, if exploring computer networks is like 'surfing', it is not that surfing we remember from the cover of a Beach Boys' record. Using the Internet is more like standing in hostile water, clutching a flimsy instrument and waiting for some wave to dump you in an unexpected location further down the beach. Moreover, there are no real 'frontiers' here: no places unoccupied by others. Nunberg suggests that the geographical comparison should be less to the expansive vistas of the American West and more to the cramped and crowded streets of a medieval city – say, Venice on a foggy afternoon. However, unlike Venice, 'locations' (information sites) on the Internet keep disappearing or changing their formats each time you return to them.

The educational implication of this analysis remains the one developed in the previous section. Namely, that information is not the same as knowledge. Pupils using this network resource have to act upon the information in ways that are demanding. The questioning, navigating, and systematising that is required represent significant skills and these skills can not be taken for granted. Neither can we take for granted young children's motivation to become learners in this environment.

Of course, it will be argued that the network-based virtual school can lay claim to the label 'school' because it does genuninely address the problems I am identifying. It does set out to create the community resources that serve to motivate, support and interpret learners' explorations. In particular, it may be argued, there are other people on networks, and their presence offers various forms of coordination and collaboration that pupils need. I believe that social context certainly will be necesary to networked learners. We know this from studies of what happens in families where a computer has been purchased partly to support the educational interests of their children. Research by Joseph Giacquinta (Giacquinta, Bauer and Levin, 1993) reveals that such children make very little use of their computers for educational purposes. It is speculated that what such reluctant learners need is some form of social scaffolding to support their computer activity. Perhaps this is just what might be added by plugging domestic computers into an internet-type structure – with all its possibilities for communication and collaborative exchange with others similarly connected. At least, this is the assumption of those who predict an imminent revolution for schooling: an impact provoked by the marriage of multi-media computing with telecommunications.

Directions for research

The above remarks leave our discussion somewhat suspended. Confident expectations for a radical transformation of schools have not been proposed here. A revolutionary future seems to depend upon whether certain forms of technology-mediated social arrangement might happen. In particular, virtual educational communities might be created as a by-product of interactions within computer networks. It would be helpful to have research that gave some indication of what was involved in fostering such possibilities. In my own work, I have tried to approach this issue by creating a modest version of the kind of virtual schooling we are entertaining here. Specifically, I have studied the consequences for a traditional undergraduate constituency of creating extensive access to computer-mediated communication. The experience of this exercise suggests that achieving self-supporting collaborative and tutorial structures through computer networks is far from easy. It is not that students fail to make use of the communicative possibilities: the problem is one of recruiting these uses towards educational goals.

I believe the obstacles to productive educational communication in these environments arise partly from a simple lack of experience with computer-mediated communication and the special forms of coordination that it supports. Consequently a further research interest of my own has involved establishing in a (primary) school setting a level of networking that is more 'local'. By this I mean a networking infrastructure that is more gently and seamlessly integrated with the existing culture of activity within the school community. I believe that any effective steps towards more radical forms of virtual schooling will emerge from experience within what might be termed 'transition environments'. The local network is such a case. It characterises the kind of working environment that is continuous with something already well known and yet which introduces the core practices of a more radical reorganisation.

A critical feature of any futuristic virtual schooling will be the shifting of educational activity away from schools as distinctly separate premises towards a more domestic base. Resources will become accessible from the linking of learners' homes to educational computer networks. While some of the social support for learning might then derive from computer-mediated interaction within the virtual school community, we may anticipate that a greater potential involvement of pupils' immediate family in the learning support process will also become important. It has long been recognised that parental involvement in joint routines of reading and problem solving is something that is very relevant to children's adaption to, and progress in school. The challenge now is to anticipate how computer-based learning resources can effectively enter into, say, parent–child exchanges in ways that are productive – as books enter into joint reading in many families at present. At Durham University, Alexandra Buxton and I have been looking at such interactions as they are mediated by educational activities available on new CD–I interactive TV technology. It is clear that the medium does furnish a rich setting for animated exchanges and that such informal social processes might come to play an increasingly important role in defining the potency of a child's early learning experiences.

Conclusions

In the last section I mentioned just three research themes that happen to be drawn from my own interests but which I think do illustrate the possibility of useful investigations in this area. I hope the rest of the discussion in this paper encourages the idea that a sound research base for future practice is urgently needed. The marriage of multi-media resources and telecommunications is a highly significant development. Yet, whether it will 'blow away' the school in the near future remains hard to judge. Its revolutionary promise arises from acting to change the very fabric of school life – to change the medium in which educational communication is supported. Such radical transformations would not normally occur by simply bolting these new possibilities on to existing social structures. It is not that, in principle, learning could not be effectively promoted within the terms of a virtual school: the question will be how comfortable people feel with the roles and expectations associated with being a virtual pupil. This, in turn, will depend upon how far the technology reconfigures other familiar arenas in which people act and exchange. In short, such drastic transformation of schooling is unlikely to happen independently of parallel transformations in the surrounding culture of trade, recreation and social life. But such transformations may well be upon us.

Getting the best out of computer technology in primary schools

Helen Rickards

The following paper outlines some examples of practical activities with computers undertaken in two primary schools. Primary practice has been influenced over past years by various schools of thought. The behaviourist approach broke down tasks into achievable steps and rewarded success. The computer was able to do this for individuals, working through specific activities suited to particular abilities. The constructivist approach perceived the learner as a discoverer. The computer could stimulate and support the learner in their attempts to construct meaning from activities. In the 1980s an example of how the computer was used in this way was Logo, devised by Papert (Papert, 1982). Logo is a programming language which young children can use and is a method of drawing lines called turtle graphics.

However, the potential independence of machine-based learning, with pupils spending the day plugged into their individual computer, awoke fears of dehumanising the future for education. Light (Scrimshaw, 1993) describes how many of the more negative images of the computer associate it with the replacement of educational experience grounded in social interaction by a technologically controlled environment. A tension exists between a vision of education as a fundamentally cooperative venture and one framed in terms of individual survival in a competitive world.

I would like to look at how IT in schools has developed. There is now greater interest in what goes on between learners and how this social interaction can be crucial to the learning process. The computer has shown that it can lead to greater development of collaborative approaches to learning and to 'quality' learning experiences.

What are the perceived benefits of using computers with small groups of pupils in school and how does this experience relate to research undertaken in the field? IT work undertaken in school is guided by the National Curriculum orders for IT which, together with support materials from NCET, focus on quality IT activities for pupils. Examples of this might be designing and constructing a model and then controlling the model through the computer or constructing a database to record information collected for a particular purpose. It is important to note that the 'drill and practice' type programs are not advocated as a 'quality' IT experience although they may be useful in supporting particular concepts in primary settings, such as spelling skills.

Control technology is one of the key areas of experience for pupils. The use of the computer to control models encourages children to solve practical problems and helps them to develop understanding in the ways systems may be controlled and how they might work more effectively. In Key Stage 2 at Morley Memorial Primary School, pupils use the computer to control simple models that they have designed and built themselves. One class built fairground models with technical lego and then wrote a program to control their movement. The pupils worked in threes. There were animated discussions throughout the project, stimulated by the problems that arose. One group of three built a ferris wheel that would not turn 360 degrees because it was too heavy. The problem had to be solved and so the children thought of a new design. At times the programs that the pupils had written did not make the models behave as the pupils thought they should and so the program was reviewed, changed (debugged!) and tested again. This type of activity requires the pupils to work collaboratively and discuss real problems. Pupils show high levels of motivation and are encouraged to apply new vocabulary required by the control program. The activities are progressive and groups can build upon their successes and apply previously learned concepts to new projects. Activities might range in complexity from simply controlling a buzzer to switch on and off, to controlling a set of traffic lights. A longer project might be to work out a defence system for a castle using sensors and switches. A considerable amount of the work in some cases would be away from the computer, for example planning, discussing and building models.

Word processing packages are the most frequently used type of software in primary schools (DFEE, 1995) and can be a source of rich discussions if used appropriately. Collaborative writing in pairs can encourage pupils to discuss their ideas and work. Word processing packages can encourage higher order writing skills such as scan reading and the close scrutiny of text. Redrafting on a computer takes away the time-consuming task of copying out text, which for some pupils is an onerous task that does little to motivate them on future occasions. Pupils are working as real writers and have access to professional fonts and methods of layout.

A particular type of word processor has been effective with pupils experiencing specific difficulties with writing at Morley. It is a 'whole word' word processor that can 'speak' as pupils enter text. The children can have a tailor-made word bank on the screen. For some of our pupils this may consist of high frequency words, whilst for others the word bank may be specific to a subject, for example the vocabulary associated with spinning wool, which was part of an Anglo-Saxon project. The pupil can click onto a word with the mouse and it will appear on the page of writing on the screen whilst the computer 'speaks' the word simultaneously. This program proved its worth when one eight-year-old boy with very specific writing difficulties wrote an imaginative and lengthy story (two pages of A4) with the word processor. He had previously laboured intensely to write by hand less than five sentences in an hour-long session. Not only had the computer given him the means to tell his story, it had also presented the work attractively so that he could share it with the class, since his own handwriting is virtually illegible. This is not to say that he should not strive to improve his handwriting, but it would be a very sad situation if he were to be denied the taste of success because his specific difficulties prevent him from demonstrating and sharing his imaginative skills with others.

Data handling skills are another main thrust of the National Curriculum orders. Pupils are encouraged to interrogate ready prepared databases and spreadsheets and to progress into constructing their own. These activities are likely to be more motivating and meaningful if they form part of a project that is engaging the pupils' interest. Some of our pupils are currently working with a prepared 'Tudor Times' database which will act as a model for building their own at a later date. The data handling activities provide a means of extending their communications skills: precision is needed when asking questions both at the design and interrogation stage. In addition the database helps to extend the mathematical skills of classifying and interpreting graphical information. The pupils are freed from the lengthy procedure of drawing graphs by hand and are given more time to practice the higher order skills of interpreting them.

One key area of interest in IT is multi-media. This is where graphics, text, video, animation or sound are combined, either with or without the computer. Hypermedia is a type of multi-media which, of necessity, involves the computer. Genesis is a hypermedia environment which allows pupils to create their own 'applications'. An application consists of several pages that are linked in particular ways. Each page contains several areas called frames. Each of these may have information attached to them, such as text, graphics or an animated sequence. Movement is achieved via links from these frames. Research undertaken through Project Horizon (NCET) and by myself with pupils experiencing mild learning difficulties has highlighted some of the benefits available. High levels of motivation appeared to enhance the quality of pupils' work and pupils were motivated by the exciting finished product. This type of software demands reflection on what has been done, as well as recording and refinement through discussion. The pupils also have to apply previously learned skills in order to construct the application: an application might consist of text, graphics, sound and animation files made in other programs.

Finally, there is the issue of the so-called 'drill and practice' type programs that are content specific. Whilst they do not constitute particularly high quality IT experiences, they are popular and useful sometimes for supporting certain parts of the curriculum. Johnson, Johnson and Stanne (Light, 1993) reported how cooperative learning situations were likely to be more effective than competitive ones. These programs are therefore likely to be more effective if pupils play two against two rather than one against one as discussion about strategies are likely to proliferate. Crooke (Light, 1993) found that of the 'game' type programs, adventure games provided the richest forum for discussion.

To conclude, there are certain key issues arising from these examples of classroom practice. Firstly, pupils' experiences are being directed towards fewer, more powerful content-free programs and these experiences are requiring pupils to use more higher order cognitive skills such as discussing, interpreting, editing and refining. The vicinity of the computer nearly always appears to be one of animated discussion which supports the opinion that the computer can and does encourage social interaction although consideration needs to be given to the types of pupil groupings at the computer. Secondly, pupils' learning appears to be enhanced when discussion of a high quality is valued and encouraged through appropriate activities and when time away from the computer is made available to plan, discuss, prepare and review work.

Getting the best out of computer technology in secondary schools

Colin Wells

Introduction

The effectiveness of children's learning at school is concerned with the quality of the experience in which they are involved, and not fundamentally about the level of sophistication of the resources used, nor how up to date these resources are. When considering any quality learning activity it is important to start from the child's particular needs and to provide appropriate resources that create a rich learning environment. This may or may not involve computers and, if it does, may or may not involve sophisticated, modern, high profile applications. The theme of this paper is therefore the involvement of appropriate computer technology in quality learning in schools. The examples and illustrations I will use will be drawn mainly from secondary schools.

Quality learning with IT

Much developmental work has been undertaken recently to consider the quality of school activities in IT. For example, in 1990, Reg North of the University of Ulster produced a book for school IT Coordinators (North, 1990) in which he proposed several relevant indicators for quality IT experiences:

- experiences which are purposeful, meaningful, relevant and which meet real needs;
- experiences which are largely practical and which involve pupils actively in IT;
- cooperative working situations, and those involving the freedom of autonomous working;
- the involvement of the teacher as a fellow pupil;
- activities which promote discussion;

- experiences which allow an iterative or investigative approach;
- experiences which aid the acquisition of information skills or the transfer of competencies;
- activities which are progressive in demands from IT as well as from the subject involved.

More recently the National Association of Advisers for Computers in Education (NAACE) and National Council for Educational Technology (NCET) produced a very useful book entitled *Reviewing IT* (NCET, 1994a) which contains considerable discussion about quality factors in IT, and concludes that where the quality of learning with or about IT is good, the effects are likely to be that pupils:

- show a greater willingness to pose questions;
- show a greater willingness to look for answers;
- show a greater willingness to take risks (in study and exploration);
- use a broader range of resources and media;
- show an ability to learn by iteration rather than through one single attempt;
- show a more positive attitude to work;
- collaborate on tasks to produce outcomes and use IT to facilitate such collaboration.

The British Computer Society Schools Committee has prepared a booklet (British Computer Society, 1996), building on the ideas of both of these publications as well as other experiences. This gives further practical guidance for teachers on how to provide quality experiences involving IT, through discussion of a range of example situations.

Valuable research evidence for the benefits of such activities can be found in articles in journals such as the *Journal of Computer Assisted Learning*. A very useful summary of such research has been compiled in the publication *IT Works* (NCET, 1994b). This includes summaries of evidence for benefits for learning, showing that:

- IT can provide a safe and non-threatening environment for learning;
- IT has the flexibility to meet the individual needs and abilities of each student;
- students who have not enjoyed learning can be encouraged by the use of IT;

- IT gives students immediate access to richer source materials;
- IT removes the chore of processing data manually and frees students to concentrate on its interpretation and use;
- interactive technology motivates and stimulates learning;
- computer simulations encourage analytical and divergent thinking;
- computers help students to learn when used in well-designed, meaningful tasks and activities.

This last point takes us back to our theme of the quality of educational IT activities.

Illustrations of quality IT activities and associated factors

In order to provide some kind of overview of the factors needed for quality activities in IT in schools, a brief selection of IT activities from schools is presented below. These are drawn from experiences in a range of schools, or reported in books, papers and magazines about IT in schools over the last few years.

Maths

- Using a simple database program to plan, carry out and display in bar chart form an investigation into traffic levels near the school.

- Using spreadsheets to model and plan the various facets of the school tuck shop, including stock levels, pricing, profits and staff costs.

Physical education

- Using a spreadsheet to plan the fixtures in a local school netball league, and record and display the results.

- Monitoring performance of heart rate connected with various exercises, both during and after, for children with various levels of fitness, and the production of graphical results.

Art

- Using a painting package to create textile designs and to experiment with different colour combinations prior to a discussion of colour mixtures suitable for various kinds of use of the material.

- Capturing pictures via a video camera, distorting/colouring them with art packages and combining them with textured embroidered versions in a collage.

Geography

- Using a program for three dimensional mapping to create a screen model of the locality around the school, to facilitate understanding of the shape of the land and conventional signs.

- Collection of a series of Meteosat images from school satellite dish for animated viewing, collection of data from automatic weather station on school roof, and comparison with synoptic charts obtained by fax from the Met Office.

Music

- Experimenting with linking pre-stored phrases of music together in various sequences using a concept keyboard, prior to pupils composing their own phrases and having clearer ideas of how to link them musically.

- Composing incidental music/sound effects for the school play, using microphone/voice input and MIDI sound editing for non-instrumental players, mixed as appropriate with acoustic sounds.

Science

- Using spreadsheets to show the connections between two variables measured in a scientific experiment as a prior stage to establishing the mathematical and scientific laws involved.

- Writing a suitable control program to monitor temperature in a greenhouse growing seeds for the pupils. The program adjusts the temperature by increasing ventilation as required for good growth conditions.

English

- Using a word processing program with a variety of font styles, colours and sizes to emphasise or portray words or phrases in an interesting manner for a report of a class trip.

- Creation of a multi-media interactive presentation about the school for new pupils and parents, involving still and moving video clips, scanned photos, appropriate text and helpful structure.

Design and technology

- Planning the design for a handheld maze, to be made from suitable materials afterwards.

- Computer aided design of new houses including furniture, accessories and estate layout. Production of scale model and estate agents' material for marketing.

History

- Investigating social problems of the nineteenth century by interrogating census records of the local area relating to that period.

- Search of historical material from CD–ROMs for a project, including facsimiles of original documents and maps, census records and other database material, and two- and three-dimensional pictures of historical objects.

Modern foreign languages

- Using a text disclosure program in French to help develop an understanding about verb endings, using a passage entered by the teacher concerning a recent school trip.

- E–mail communications link with the relevant foreign country – collaborating in the production of a joint newspaper involving news in both languages.

Frequently occurring factors

A number of factors occur in these examples which contribute to the potential success of the activity. The activities:

- are relevant to the children;
- motivate the children;
- are useful to the children or to others;
- are creative, or solve a real problem;
- involve cooperation with other people;
- involve making comparisons or providing multidimensional views on situations;
- integrate IT appropriately with other methods.

Conclusions

The factors listed above may seem basic and obvious, but they enable children to use IT as an effective learning tool. Hence when planning IT activities for and with children, a short time considering such factors could easily result in significant improvements in the activities offered and move further towards getting the best out of computer technology.

Conclusions

Tim Gill

Much of the debate about children and new technology can be framed around a single powerful image: the image of a solitary child, face lit only by the light from the screen, completely at the mercy of the images being transmitted. Children spend one third of their free time in front of a screen (based on figures from *Social Trends*, Central Statistical Office, 1995). Add to this the growing use of computers in schools, and it is hard to resist the idea that technology is somehow 'stealing our babies' souls', as Libby Purves puts it in her contribution to this book.

Yet there is much that is missing from this image of new technology as an electronic Pied Piper. For one thing, adults do not feature in it at all. (Perhaps this in part explains our alarm – we fear that machines are destined to replace us not just as workers but even as parents and carers.) If we as adults are better to understand the developing relationship between children and technology, we must also recognise our own part in the picture: our relation to technology and our relation to children.

Technological innovations provoke deep fears in adults – one has only to think of Frankenstein, or the Luddites. We fear that computers will make us obsolete, or worse. Elizabeth Dwomoh from Graveney Secondary School asked her friends about their greatest fears concerning new technology. In reply, 'nearly all of them said it was the fact that computers were replacing more and more humans in industry'. Whether or not this is true, it is a deep fear. And behind it lies an even deeper one, expressed in a rhetorical question from Elizabeth:

> 'Will there come a time when humankind is run by computers, instead of being run by man? Is there a possibility that one day man's innermost being will be known as a result of computers?'

But technology also excites us, for it presents us with new challenges and possibilities. This excitement is most visible in the debate about the Internet, complete with its surfing and Wild West imagery (metaphors pointedly questioned by Crook). Some children share this excitement; Natasha Mudhar from Graveney School is 'completely convinced by computers'. She explains why:

> 'I don't use the computer for playing games but for word processing, writing poems, stories and many other things. At school I use it for spreadsheets, word processing and graphics. I think that computers are excellent.'

But other children may not share these fears and hopes, and we must be careful not to misinterpret children's experiences. As Elizabeth Dwomoh puts it:

> 'I was born in the computer age, so it is very hard for me to say if the computer has been a good influence on society as a whole, because I have nothing to compare it to.'

Adults also have a complex relationship with children and childhood, which can in turn complicate our understanding of children themselves. We use many different models in thinking about children, their behaviour and their experiences. Some models depict children as being like animals, who have to be forcibly trained to behave in ways acceptable to adult society. Others highlight children's weaknesses and deficits (physical, emotional and mental) compared to adults. Others emphasise children's autonomy and their ability to adapt. Each of these models offers its own insights, but each has its drawbacks. (This issue is usefully discussed in the context of supervised play services in Petrie, 1994.) The danger is that we as adults start to use one of these models as if it encapsulates the whole truth about the nature of children. When this happens, we are liable to obscure important aspects of children's own experience. Even those of us who work professionally with or for children find it easier to conceive of them as adults-in-waiting than as human beings with their own views on leisure and education. Of course, we cannot deny that children's engagement with new technology may do them harm. We do not allow children the same autonomy, or grant them the same freedom of choice, as adults. Nor should we. But we should recognise children's abilities and interests, and encourage them to make decisions and choices themselves on the basis of these abilities. As the pupils from Graveney School show, children have their own views and opinions about new technology.

In the light of this, we may be underestimating the complexity of children's engagement with technology. While the violence and gender stereotyping in television, videos and computer games can be disturbing, perhaps children themselves do not buy into the world-view on offer quite so unquestioningly as Stutz or Newson suggest.

In her description of video games, Stutz ignores the existence of a range of game genres, as outlined by Griffiths. These make a big difference to children's attitudes, as the quotes from Graveney pupils show. Libby Purves's enthusiasm for the game 'Sim City' suggests that Stutz may not have to look too far in her search for 'a fresh kind of game in which the players are set a variety of life-affirming tasks'.

Newson's argument makes an explicit link between the level of television and video violence and the murder of James Bulger. Newson is right to insist that we try to understand what led two young boys to abduct, torture and kill a two-year-old toddler. The danger is that this intense need for explanation can produce oversimplified or even wrong answers. Child murderers are extremely rare, and furthermore not a new phenomenon; Gitta Seveny in her study of Mary Bell, another child murderer, estimates that in the UK there have been just 27 cases in the last 250 years (Seveny, 1995). In the Bulger case there is at best ambiguous evidence of any link with videos (see for instance the discussion in Smith, 1995). So it may be premature to rest so much of one's argument on one case, in advance of the 'careful collection of case history and material' that Newson advocates. The challenge for researchers is to ensure that this research takes a sophisticated approach to factors that may prove to be relevant, including the family, social and environmental conditions of children. And the challenge for parents and other adults who influence children's leisure activities (such as providers of after-school clubs and other supervised play services) is to become more familiar with the programmes and games that are on offer. Developing a dialogue with children, whether at home or in school, will help to allay our fears and may make it easier to resolve conflicts with children over their leisure activities.

Interestingly, children themselves are worried about what they watch, and do believe that video and television violence are 'bad for children's health and behaviour' as Natalie Blackburne from Graveney School put it. However, children tend to displace these effects on to children younger than themselves. Natalie herself, after describing the effect on her two-year-old cousin of watching 'Power Rangers', asks: 'If this is what is happening to a two-year-old in 1995, who is to say that this will not be happening to a one-year old in the year 2000?' And Julian Wood, a researcher who has worked with the British Board of Film Classification, identifies the same displacement occurring (Wood, 1993).

Many adults agree with Natalie about the effects of television and video watching, and argue for greater restrictions on viewing. This is not the place for a detailed discussion of the pros and cons of censorship, or of the classification system for videos in the UK. However, it is worth highlighting that children themselves see the classifications as, in Allerton's words, 'making material attractive...by giving it the status of forbidden fruit'. Wood observed the same phenomenon in a group of boys watching a 'horror' video (Wood, 1993). This is not an argument against classification systems, which as Allerton shows do provide useful information for parents (increasingly supplemented by more information about the content of videos, as with a voluntary labelling initiative introduced in 1995). Rather it shows the need, as Allerton argues, for educational initiatives aimed at both parents and children which encourage children to manage their viewing and parents to feel supported in their regulation of it.

We need to step back in another way from the image of the electronic Pied Piper if we are to get a better picture of how children are engaging with new technology. In addition to putting ourselves in the picture as adults – as parents, teachers, researchers, play or child care professionals – we also need to take account of the context of the engagement, of its place in children's lives.

Consider how children are spending their leisure time. 1995 saw at least four murders of children, apparently by strangers, at the start of the summer vacation. Around the same time, two of the UK's largest children's charities, Barnardos and Save the Children Fund, both published reports highlighting the lack of safe places for children to play. Indeed Barnardos found that 85 per cent of parents felt that their children were less safe outside than they themselves were as children (McNeish and Roberts, 1995). Whatever we feel about the justifications or reasons for these fears and beliefs, it is hardly surprising that computer games are being bought in huge numbers by parents anxious to offer their children something to do. British children spend nearly 20 hours a week watching television and videos, according to *Social Trends* (Central Statistical Office, 1995). But when you ask children what they like doing, as Leicester City Council did, it seems that 'children are not necessarily watching a lot of TV because it's their absolutely favourite thing to do' (Leicester City Council, 1993). Rather, as with computer games, children often watch television to fill the time, or because there is nothing better to do. For instance, the Leicester City Council survey found that 94 per cent of children want to play outdoors more. In another piece of research (Phillips and others, 1995), schoolchildren were asked why they played computer games; 34 per cent said 'to pass the time' and 12 per cent 'to avoid doing other things'. So if we want children to watch less television and play computer games less, we need to find them better things to do, for the sake of their physical as well as mental health (for expressions of concern about children's fitness levels, see *More People, More Active, More Often: Physical Activity in England*, Department of Health, 1995). Few would disagree with Stutz's arguments for the importance of what she calls 'real play': the collaborative, active games that children play outside of their homes. The problem is that the outdoors – historically both the site and the raw material for much of children's play – is now out-of-bounds for many children, especially if they want to play somewhere away from adults. Parental fears about crime and traffic accidents have severely restricted children's independent mobility (see Hillman, Adams and Whitelegg, 1990). In this context, the popularity of computer games is not so surprising.

One delegate at the 'Electronic Children' conference claimed that James Bulger would never have been killed if there had been a good adventure playground in the neighbourhood. This is a strong claim for the therapeutic value of play. But in trying to evaluate such a claim, we lack even the basic data to judge the consequences of the restrictions we place on children. Meanwhile, a generation of children is growing up without the play experiences that many adults took for granted in their own childhood. So there is a real need for comparative and longitudinal research into the social and physical consequences of different types of play experiences.

If we ask how new technology is being used in education, the image of computers stealing our children's souls holds less sway. There is widespread support for the need to introduce children to such a vital business and educational tool. Indeed, Department for Education and Employment figures show a dramatic growth in school use of computers over the period from 1985 to 1994. For instance, in secondary schools there were ten pupils for every computer in 1994, compared to 60 for every computer in 1985 (DFEE, 1995). Total expenditure on information technology in secondary schools has grown from £9.8 million to £86.9 million over the same period. And the figures tell the same story in primary and special schools. According to the DFEE, in 1993/4 56 per cent of teaching staff in primary schools used computers at least twice a week. Computers are also used as learning tools at home, although figures for use are harder to find. Most of our pupils from Graveney School use computers in their homework, perhaps writing work using a word processor or researching topics with a CD–ROM resource.

As to the impact of computers in education, the picture is confused. Educationalists, teachers and pupils all agree that computers benefit children's education. This enthusiasm is in part simply a recognition of the advantages of early familiarisation with technology. Times are changing, as Debbie Lovell from Graveney School observes:

> 'My mum first saw a computer in her early twenties, I first saw a computer when I was eight years old, and if I were to have children it is possible that they might even learn to read and write on a computer.'

Pupils also benefit because of their motivation to use computers. As we have seen, one of the most important consequences of the introduction of new technology into classrooms has been the re-emergence of progressive teaching practices, themselves the target of political criticism since the 1980s. Given the original rationale for these styles of teaching, it is no surprise that children are better motivated in classes that use computers. But this may be less to do with the intrinsic advantages of the technology than with a synthesis of novelty and progressive teaching practices.

The growth in communications technology is set to raise further questions about children's access to, and use of, technology. Crook argues that it is developments of this kind that are most likely to lead to fundamental changes in educational practice. But as Libby Purves notes, the Internet is also a cause for concern, with its potential for easy access to violent or pornographic material. At the time of writing, comparatively few children have access to the Internet, and it may be too early to assess how they are engaging with it. But it is already clear that the lessons learnt from children's use of videos and computer games will also be relevant here.

Perhaps the central message of this book is that children's engagement with new technology cannot be considered in a vacuum. What we need, and what this book aims to provide, is an overview of how boys and girls from a range of backgrounds are actually engaging with new technology – what the processes mean to them as children and to us as adults, what they (and we) are gaining and losing. Of course we must develop children's capacities, and protect children from harm. But we must do so imaginatively. This means respecting children's abilities and wishes. It means remembering that the landscape we are surveying includes much more than a child staring at a screen. It means understanding the world from the point of view of children, and listening to their experience. Because each child has only one childhood.

References

Allerton, M (1995) 'Emotions and coping: children's talk about negative emotional responses to television', *Early Child Development and Care*, 109, 1–22

Anderson, C A and Ford, C M (1986) 'Affect of the game player: short term effects of highly and mildly aggressive video games', *Personality and Social Psychology Bulletin*, 12, 390–402

Andison, F S (1977) 'TV violence and viewer aggression: a cumulation of study results', *Public Opinion Quarterly*, 41, 314–31

Atari (1982) *A public perspective*. US, California: Author

Bailey, S M (1993) *Criminal Justice Matters*, 6–7

Barlow, G and Hill, A eds (1985) *Video Violence and Children*. Hodder and Stoughton

Bazalgette, C and Buckingham, D (1995) *in* the Introduction to Bazalgette, C and Buckingham, D eds *In Front of the Children: Screen Entertainment and Young Audiences*. British Film Institute

Berkowicz, L (1970) 'The contagion of violence: an S–R mediational analysis of some of the effects of observed aggression' *in* Arnold, W J and Page, M M eds *Nebraska Symposium on Motivation*. US, Lincoln: University of Nebraska Press

Belson, W (1978) *Television Violence and the Adolescent Boy*. Saxon House

Bettelheim, B (1975) *The Uses of Enchantment: The Meaning and Importance of Fairy Tales and Legends*. Penguin

Billington, M (1994) 'A little blood goes a long way', *Guardian*, 20 April

Bonel, P (1993) *Playing for Real*. National Children's Play and Recreation Unit

Bowman, R P and Rotter, J C (1983) 'Computer games: friend or foe?', *Elementary School Guidance and Counselling*, 18, 25–34

Brasington, R (1990) 'Nintendinitis', *New England Journal of Medicine*, 322, 1473–4

Braun, C M J and others (1986) 'Adolescents and microcomputers: sex differences, proxemics, task and stimulus variables', *Journal of Psychology*, 120, 529–42

Briggs, K M (1977) *British FolkTales and Legends: A Sampler.* Granada Publishing

Bright, D A and Bringhurst, D C (1992) 'Nintendo elbow', *Western Journal of Medicine*, 156, 667–8

Brown, R I F (1989) 'Gaming, gambling, risk taking, addictions and a developmental model of a pathology of man–machine relationships' *in* Klabbers, J and others eds *Simulation Gaming*. Pergamon

British Computer Society Schools Committee (1996) *Developing Quality IT*. British Computer Society

Buckingham, D (1993) *Children Talking Television: the Development of Television Literacy*. Falmer Press

Buckingham, D (1996) *Moving Images: Understanding Children's Emotional Responses to Television*. Manchester University Press

Buckingham, D and Allerton, M (1996) *A Review of Research on Children's Negative Emotional Responses to Television* (Broadcasting Standards Council Research Paper)

Butterfield, F (1983) 'Video game specialists come to praise Pacman, not bury him', *New York Times*, 24 May (p22)

Calouste Gulbenkian Foundation (1995) *Children and Violence: Report of the Commission on Children and Violence Convened by the Calouste Gulbenkian Foundation*. Calouste Gulbenkian Foundation

Carter, R C, Kennedy, R S and Bittner, A C (1980, October) *Selection of performance evaluation tests for environmental research* (Paper given at the 24th Annual Meeting of the Human Factors Society)

Casanova, J and Casanova, J (1991) 'Nintendinitis', *Journal of Hand Surgery*, 16, 181

Central Statistical Office (1995) *Social Trends*. HMSO

Chaffin, J D, Maxwell, B and Thompson, B (1982) 'ARC–ED curriculum: the application of video game formats to educational software', *Exceptional Children*, 49, 173–8

Comstock, G (1991) *Television and the American Child*. US, San Diego, California: Academic Press

Cooper, J and Mackie, D (1986) 'Video games and aggression in children', *Journal of Applied Social Psychology*, 16, 726–44

Corkery, J C (1990) 'Nintendo power', *American Journal of Diseases in Children*, 144, 959

Creasey, G L and Myers, B J (1986) 'Video games and children: effects in leisure activities, schoolwork and peer involvement', *Merrill-Palmer Quarterly*, 32, 251–62

Crook, C K (1987) *Computers, Cognition and Development*. Wiley

Crook, C K (1994a) 'Electronic communications in two educational settings: some theory and practice' *in* O'Malley, C ed. *Computer-supportive collaborative learning*. Springer

Crook, C K (1994b) *Computers and the Collaborative Experience of Learning*. Routledge

Cuban, L (1986) *Teachers and Machines*. US, New York: Teachers College

Cumberbatch, G and Howitt, D (1989) *A Measure of Uncertainty: The Effects of the Mass Media* (Broadcasting Standards Council Research Monograph). John Libbey

Cunningham, H (1995) 'Mortal Kombat and Computer Game Girls' *in* Bazalgette, C and Buckingham, D eds *In Front of the Children: Screen Entertainment and Young Audiences*. British Film Institute

Dalquist, N R, Mellinger, J F and Klass, D W (1983) 'Hazards of video games in patients with light-sensitive epilepsy', *Journal of the American Medical Association*, 249, 776–77

Department for Education and Employment (1995) *Statistical Bulletin: Survey of Information Technology in Schools*. Department for Education and Employment

Department of Health (1995) *More People, More Active, More Often: Physical Activity in England*. Department of Health

Dominick, J R (1984) 'Videogames, television violence and aggression in teenagers', *Journal of Communication*, 34, 136–147

Economist Intelligence Unit (1991) Press release

Egli, E A and Meyers, L S (1984) 'The role of video game playing in adolescent life: is there a reason to be concerned?', *Bulletin of the Psychonomic Society*, 22, 309–12

Eron, L D (1982) 'Parent–child interaction, television violence, and aggression of children', *American Psychologist*, 37, 197–211

Farrington, D P (1994) The influence of the family on delinquent development (Paper given at Crime and the Family conference). Family Policy Studies Centre

Favaro, P J (1982) 'Games for cooperation and growth – an alternative for designers', *Softside*, 6, 18–21

Favaro, P J (1984) 'How video games affect players', *Softside*, 7, 16–17

Freud, A (1928) *Introduction to the Technique of Child Analysis* (Clark, L P trans.). US, New York: Nervous and Mental Disease Publishing

Friedland, R P and St John, J N (1984) 'Video-game palsy: distal ulnar neuropathy in a video game enthusiast', *New England Journal of Medicine*, 311, 58–9

Gallup, G (1982) 'The typical American teenager', *Seattle Times*, 19 May (p17)

Gardner, J E (1991) 'Can the Mario Bros help? Nintendo games as an adjunct in psychotherapy with children', *Psychotherapy*, 28, 667–70

Gauntlett, D (1995) *Moving Experiences: Understanding Television's Influences and Effects*. John Libbey

Giacquinta, J B, Bauer, J A and Levin, J E (1993) *Beyond Technology's Promise*. Cambridge University Press

Gill, T R (1995) *Playing for Local Government*. National Children's Bureau

Graham, J (1988) *Amusement machines: dependency and delinquency*. Home Office Research Study No. 101. HMSO

Greenfield, P 'Video games and cognitive skills' *in* Baughman, S S and Claggett, P D eds (1983) *Video Games and Human Development: A Research Agenda for the 80s*. US Cambridge, Massachusetts: Harvard Graduate School of Education

Greenfield P (1984) *Media and the Mind of the Child: From Print to Television, Video Games and Computers*. US, Cambridge, Massachusetts: Harvard University Press

Griffiths, M D (1991a) 'Amusement machine playing in childhood and adolescence: a comparative analysis of video games and fruit machines', *Journal of Adolescence*, 14, 53–73

Griffiths, M D (1991b) 'The observational analysis of adolescent gambling in UK amusement arcades', *Journal of Community and Applied Social Psychology*, 1, 309–20

Griffiths, M D (1991c) 'Adolescent fruit machine use: a review of current issues and trends', *UK Forum on Young People and Gambling Newsletter*, 4, 2–3

Griffiths, M D (1991d) 'Fruit machine addiction: two brief case studies', *British Journal of Addiction*, 86, 465

Griffiths, M D (1992) 'Pinball wizard: a case study of a pinball addict', *Psychological Reports*, 71, 160–2

Griffiths, M D (1993) 'Are computer games bad for children?', *The Psychologist: Bulletin of the British Psychological Society*, 6, 401–7

Griffiths, M D (1994) 'The role of cognitive bias and skill in fruit machine gambling', *British Journal of Psychology*, 85, 351–89

Griffiths, M D (1995) *Adolescent Gambling*. Routledge

Griffiths, M D (forthcoming) *Technological Addictions*. Routledge

Griffiths, M D and Hunt, N (1993, December) *The acquisition, development and maintenance of computer game playing in adolescence* (Paper presented at the British Psychological Society London Conference, City University)

Griffiths, M D and Hunt, N (1995) 'Computer game playing in adolescence: prevalence and demographic indicators', *Journal of Community and Applied Social Psychology*, 5, 189–94

Grunfeld, F F (1982) Swiss Committee for UNICEF

Gutman, D (1982) 'Video games wars', *Video Game Player*, Fall (Whole issue)

Hart, E J (1990) 'Nintendo epilepsy', *New England Journal of Medicine*, 322, 1473

Hillman, M, Adams, J and Whitelegg, J (1990) *One False Move: A Study of Children's Independent Mobility*. Policy Studies Institute

Homer, S (1992) 'Switch on and take over the world', *Independent*, 21 December (p15)

Homer, S (1993) 'Electronic code can programme children's viewing', *Independent*, 11 January (p1)

Hubbard, P (1991) 'Evaluating computer games for language learning', *Simulation and Gaming*, 22, 220–23

Huesmann, L R and Eron, L D (1986) *Television and the Aggressive Child: A Cross-National Comparison*. US, Hilldale, New Jersey: Lawrence Erlbaum Associates

Huesmann, L R and others (1983) *Aggression and its Correlates over 22 years*. US, Chicago: University of Illinois

Itzin, C (1991) *Pornography-Related Sexual Violence: A Review of the Evidence*, Report to the Home Office

James, O (1995) *Juvenile Violence in a Winner–Loser Culture*. Free Association Press

Jones, M B (1981) 'Differential retention and convergence with practice', *The Pennsylvania State University – 1st Quarterly Report*, MDA 903–81–C–0293

Kaplan, S J (1983) 'The image of amusement arcades and differences in male and female video game playing', *Journal of Popular Culture*, 16, 93–8

Kaplan, S J and Kaplan, S (1981) 'A research note: video games, sex, and sex differences', *Social Science*, 56, 208–12

Keepers, G A (1990) 'Pathological preoccupation with video games', *Journal of the American Academy of Child and Adolescent Psychiatry*, 29, 49–50

Kerr, P (1982) 'Should video games be restricted by law?', *New York Times*, 3 June (p8)

Kestenbaum, G I and Weinstein, L (1985) 'Personality, psychopathology, and developmental issues in male adolescent video game use', *Journal of the American Academy of Child and Adolescent Psychiatry*, 24, 325–37

Kiesler, S, Sproull, L and Eccles, J S (1983) 'Second class citizens', *Psychology Today*, 17, 3, 41–8

Kinder, M (1993) 'The Amazing Video Game Boom', *Time International*, No. 39

Klein, M (1932) *The psychoanalysis of children.* Hogarth

Klein, M H (1984) 'The bite of Pac-man', *Journal of Psychohistory*, 11, 395–401

Koop, E (1982) 'Surgeon general sees danger in video games', *New York Times*, 10 November (ppA–16)

Kuczmierczyk, A R, Walley, P B and Calhoun, K S (1987) 'Relaxation training, in vivo exposure and response-prevention in the treatment of compulsive video-game playing', *Scandinavian Journal of Behaviour Therapy*, 16, 185–90

Lazarus, R S and Folkman, S (1984) *Stress, Appraisal and Coping.* US, New York: Springer

Leerhsen, C, Zabarsky, M and McDonald, D H (1983) 'Video games zap Harvard', *Newsweek*, 6 June (p92)

Leicester City Council (1993) *Kidsdeal: Leisure Services Report.*

Lepper, M R and others (1993) 'Motivational techniques of expert human tutors: lessons for the design of computer-based tutors', *in* Lajoie, S and Derry, S eds (1993) *Computers as cognitive tools.* US, Hillsdale, New Jersey: Lawrence Erlbaum Associates

Light, P (1993) 'Collaborative learning with computers' *in* Scrimshaw, P ed. (1993) *Language, classrooms and computers.* Routledge

Loftus, G A and Loftus, E F (1983) *Mind at Play: The Psychology of Video Games.* US, New York: Basic Books

Lynch, W J (1981) *TV games as therapeutic interventions* (Paper presented at the American Psychological Association, Los Angeles)

Lynch, W J (1983) *Cognitive retraining using microcomputer games and commercially available software* (Paper presented at the Meeting of the International Neuropsychological Society, Mexico City)

Maccoby, E E and Jacklin, C N (1974) *The psychology of sex differences*. US, Stanford, California: Stanford University Press

Malone, T W (1981) 'Toward a theory of intrinsically motivating instruction', *Cognitive Science*, 4, 333–69.

McCowan, T C (1981) 'Space Invaders wrist', *New England Journal of Medicine*, 304, 1368

McIlwraith, R (1990, August) *Theories of television addiction* (Paper presented at the American Psychological Association, Boston)

McIlwraith, R and others (1991) 'Television addiction: theories and data behind the ubiquitous metaphor', *American Behavioral Scientist*, 35, 104–21

McLure, R F and Mears, F G (1984) 'Video game players: personality characteristics and demographic variables', *Psychological Reports*, 55, 271–6

McNeish, D and Roberts, H (1995) *Playing it Safe: Today's Children at Play*. Barnardos

Medved, M (1992) *Hollywood vs. America: Popular Culture and the War on Traditional Values*. Harper Collins

Microprose (1992) Press release

Milavsky, J and others (1982) *Television and Aggression: A Panel Study*. US, New York: Academic Press

Miller, D L G (1991) 'Nintendo neck', *Canadian Medical Association Journal*, 145, 1202

Mitchell, E (1985) 'The dynamics of family interaction around home video games', *Marriage and Family Review*, 8, 121–35

Morlock, H, Yando, T and Nigolean, K (1985) 'Motivation of video game players', *Psychological Reports*, 57, 247–50

National Council for Educational Technology (1994a) *Reviewing IT*. NCET

National Council for Educational Technology (1994b) *IT Works*. NCET

Nawrocki, L H and Winner, J L (1983) 'Video games: instructional potential and classification', *Journal of Computer Based Instruction*, 10, 80–2

Neustatter, A (1991) 'Keyboard junkies', *The Independent on Sunday Review*, 17 November (p64)

North, R (1990) *Managing IT: the role of the IT Coordinator*. University of Ulster

Opie, I (1994) *People in the Playground*. Oxford University Press

Papert, S (1982) *Mindstorms: Children, Computers and Powerful Ideas*. Harvester Press

Papert, S (1984) 'Trying to predict the future', *Popular Computing*, October

Petrie, P (1994) *Play and Care Out of School*. HMSO

Phillips, C and others (1995) 'Home video game playing in schoolchildren: a study of incidence and patterns of play', *Journal of Adolescence*, 18

Phillips, W R (1991) 'Video game therapy', *New England Journal of Medicine*, 325, 1056–7

Provenzo, E (1991) *Video kids: Making Sense of Nintendo*. US, Cambridge, Massachusetts: Harvard University Press

Purves, L (1986) *How Not To Be a Perfect Mother: The Crafty Mother's Guide to a Quiet Life*. Fontana

Purves, L (1991) *How Not To Be a Perfect Child*. Fontana

Purves, L (1994) *How Not To Be the Perfect Family*. Harper Collins

Reinstein, L (1983) 'de Quervain's stenosing tenosynovitis in a video games player', *Archives of Physical and Medical Rehabilitation*, 64, 434–5

Rennie, S 'Victims of Nintendo or Children Choosing?' *in* Lubelska, A ed. (1993) *Better Play*. National Children's Bureau

Roberts, J and Pool, Y (1988) *Slot machine playing by children: Results of a survey in Minehead and Taunton*. Spectrum Children's Trust

Rushton, D N (1981) '"Space Invader" epilepsy', *The Lancet*, 1, 501

Salend, S and Santora, D (1985) 'Employing access to the computer as a reinforcer for secondary students', *Behavioural Disorders*, November

Scheibe, K E and Erwin, M (1979) 'The computer as altar', *Journal of Social Psychology*, 108, 103–9.

Schink, J C (1991) 'Nintendo enuresis', *American Journal of Diseases in Children*, 145, 1094

Schneider, C (1987) *Children's Television: The Art, the Business and How it Works*. US, Chicago: NTC Business Books

Scrimshaw, P (1993) *in* the Introduction to Scrimshaw, P ed. *Language, Classrooms and Computers*. Routledge

Selnow, G W (1984) 'Playing video games: the electronic friend', *Journal of Communication*, 34, 148–56

Seveny, G (1995) *The Case of Mary Bell: A Portrait of a Child who Murdered*. Pimlico

Shotton, M (1989) *Computer addiction?: A Study of Computer Dependency*. Taylor and Francis

Siegal, I M (1991) 'Nintendonitis', *Orthopedics*, 14, 745.

Silvern, S B (1986) 'Classroom use of video games', *Education Research Quarterly*, 10, 10–16

Silvern, S B, Williamson, P A and Countermine, T A (1983, April) *Aggression in young children and video game play* (Paper presented at the Biennial meeting of the Society for Research in Child Development, Detroit)

Simon, H A (1983) 'Why should machines learn?' *in* Michalski, R ed. *Machine Learning: An Artificial Intelligence Approach*. US, Palo Alto, California: Tioga

Sims, A, and Melville-Thomas, G (1985) 'Survey of the opinion of child and adolescent psychiatrists on the viewing of violent videos by children', *Bulletin, Royal College of Psychiatrists*, 9, 238–40

Smith, D J (1995) *The Sleep of Reason: The James Bulger Case*. Arrow

Soper, W B and Miller, M J (1983) 'Junk time junkies: an emerging addiction among students', *School Counsellor*, 31, 40–3

Spence, J (1988) 'The use of computer arcade games in behaviour management', *Maladjustment and Therapeutic Education*, 6, 64–8

Strein, W and Kochman, W (1984) 'Effects of computer games on children's co-operative behaviour', *Journal of Research and Development in Education*, 18, 1

Sturrock, G (1993) 'A metaphysical journey into the meaning of Play', *International Play Journal*, 1, 1

Stutz, E (1991) *What are They Doing Now? A Study of Children aged Seven to Fourteen*. Play for Life

Suppes, P (1966) 'The uses of computers in education', *Scientific American*, 215, 207–20

Surrey, D (1982) 'It's like good training for life', *Natural History*, 91, 71–83

Szer, J (1983) 'Video games as physiotherapy', *Medical Journal of Australia*, 1, 401–2

Taylor, J and Laurillard, D (1995) 'Supporting resource based learning' *in* Heap, N and others eds *Information Technology and Society*. Sage

Trachtman, P (1981) 'A generation meets computers – and they are friendly', *Smithsonian*, 12, 6, 50–61

Turkle, S (1984) *The Second Self: Computer and the Human Spirit*. Simon and Schuster

Wartella, E (1995) 'Media and problem behaviours in young people' *in* Rutter, M and Smith, D J eds *Psychosocial Disorders in Young People: Time Trends and their Causes*. Wiley

Winston, B (1986) *Misunderstanding Media*. Routledge and Kegan Paul

Wood, J (1993) 'Repeatable pleasures' *in* Buckingham, D ed. *Reading Audiences: Young People and the Media*. Manchester University Press

Zimbardo, P (1982) 'Understanding psychological man: a state of the science report', *Psychology Today*, 16, 15

Index

Entries are arranged in letter-by-letter order (hyphens and spaces between words are ignored). Interviews with individual children are entered under the heading 'interviews'.

Becoming a member

The National Children's Bureau offers an extensive Library and Information Service – probably the largest child care information resource in the UK. We also run a comprehensive programme of conferences and seminars, and publish a wide range of books, leaflets and resource packs. In addition, the Bureau gives members the opportunity to tap into an influential network of professionals who care about children, helping to set the agenda for the nineties and beyond.

Membership of the National Children's Bureau provides you with:

- a quarterly mailing containing:
  - *Children UK*: the Bureau's journal
  - *Highlights:* briefing papers containing summaries of research findings and recent reports of legislation on relevant issues;
- access to the library and information service including databases, books, journals and periodicals;
- first access to the findings of our research and development projects;
- advance notice of our extensive programme of conferences and seminars throughout the country and concessionary prices;
- concessionary prices and advance details for Bureau publications.

The National Children's Bureau can support you in the day-to-day task of meeting the needs of children and young people. For further details please contact Jane Lewis, Membership Marketing Coordinator, National Children's Bureau, 8 Wakley Street, London EC1V 7QE or call 0171 843 6047 for further information.

Publications

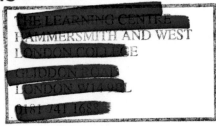

THE LEARNING CENTRE
HAMMERSMITH AND WEST
LONDON COLLEGE
GLIDDON ROAD
LONDON W14 9BL
0181 741 1688

Recent works include:

Developing Parenting Programmes

Trust Betrayed? – Munchausen syndrome by proxy, inter-agency child protection and partnership with families

Good Practice in Sex Education: A sourcebook for schools

Communication Between Babies in their first year – book and video pack

Children's Rights and HIV

Managing to Change – Training materials for staff in day care centres for young children

Schools' SEN Policies Pack

Crossing the Boundaries – A discussion of Children's Services Plans

Growing Up

It's Your Meeting!

Intervention in the Early Years

Children, Sex Education and the Law

The Bureau also publishes a quarterly journal, *Children & Society* – to subscribe please contact John Wiley & Sons, Tel: 01243 770634   Fax: 01243 770638

For further information or a catalogue please contact:
Book Sales, National Children's Bureau, 8 Wakley Street, London EC1V 7QE
Tel: 0171 843 6029   Fax: 0171 278 9512

&Children Society

Editors: Gillian Pugh, Director, Early Childhood Unit, National Children's Bureau and Nigel Parton, Professor of Child Care, University of Huddersfield

Children & Society was launched 10 years ago and is now established as the primary multidisciplinary journal for all who work with children and young people – as practitioners, managers, researchers, teachers, or concerned individuals.

A central theme of Volume 10 will be the ethics and methodology of research with children.

Articles will be published by a number of distinguished researchers including: Priscilla Alderson, Gary Craig, Mary Jane Drummond, Malcolm Hill, Berry Mayall, Martin Richards, Ruth Sinclair and John Tresiliotis.

Whatever your involvement in child care, health, education or development, Children & Society must be considered essential reading!

WILEY

NATIONAL CHILDREN'S BUREAU

EHWLC LEARNING CENTRE
EALING GREEN

LEARNING CENTRE
HAMMERSMITH AND WEST
LONDON COLLEGE
GLIDDON ROAD
LONDON W14 9BL
0181 741 1688